SYS-TAO

Western Logic ~ Eastern Flow

AN EMERGING LEADERSHIP PHILOSOPHY

BOB BROWNE

Chairman & CEO Emeritus
Great Plains Coca-Cola Bottling Company

MILLICHAP BOOKS

Published by Millichap Books
millichapbooks.com

Book & cover design by Carl Brune

Copyedited by Franklin Page

First Edition. First printing.

Printed in Canada

ISBN 978-1-937462-00-0 (casebound)

ISBN 978-1-937462-10-9 (paperbound)

ISBN 978-1-937462-21-5 (ebook)

Sys-Tao.org

Changing your mind is hard.

Changing your habits is harder.

*Changing an organization's culture
is even more difficult.*

CONTENTS

PART ONE
Background

CHAPTER ONE

CHAPTER TWO

PART TWO
Conceptual Foundations

CHAPTER THREE

CHAPTER FOUR

CHAPTER FIVE

CHAPTER SIX

CHAPTER SEVEN

CHAPTER EIGHT

CHAPTER NINE

CHAPTER TEN

PART THREE
The Principles

Foreword

It's a pleasure for me to write this foreword to my friend Bob Browne's book, *Sys-Tao*. After several years as an officer in the Navy, two years of full time study at Columbia Business School and experience at a major accounting firm one can infer Bob had received the best management training the Western world had to offer. He joined the family business, Great Plains Coca-Cola Bottling. It soon became evident that not all the heirs were happy with the existing state of affairs. With over sixty heirs at different stages of life unanimity was rare. Some wanted more income, some wanted to cash out their shares.

So Bob brought in some investors and together they did a leveraged buy-out of the company, although at the time he was unfamiliar with the term. They invested $7.5 million of their own money to buy the company in 1980. In December of 2011 they sold the company to Coca-Cola for $364 million. A tidy return. In the meantime the company was profitable, paid off debt, provided employment in the community, paid respectable salaries, and paid dividends to the owners. Were the aim to sell as many copies as possible in today's business book market, the title could have been: $7.5 to $364 Million: How I transformed a small family business into a world leader and made a fortune; or some such title. But this is much more than a how-to book on running a successful company and making an atypical return.

But to continue with the progression of the story, the former owners were paid $45 million, which means Bob and his investors had to borrow $37.5 million. Bob was now in charge. Debt and being in charge have a way of focusing one's attention. So Bob embarked on improving the results of the company. He did everything he had been taught to do in the elite school from which he had graduated, the prestigious accounting firm he had worked for and at the US Navy. Targets and goals were made and progressively raised. And for a while results did improve. But he ran into a major obstacle of disgruntled workers who were being pushed for greater results. The mantra of much of management thinking, taught in business schools at the time, and still taught in many schools and practiced in many companies, can be summarized as have others work harder; listen to employees (maybe) but then ignore what they say. It is management against employees.

The obstacle revealed itself as the Teamsters Union coming in and making an effort to unionize the plant. While the Teamsters were defeated they may deserve some credit here as Bob had to rethink management. But the same thing happens at other companies with a much poorer resolution. One thing was different. Bob had a gnawing feeling, even as results were improving, that something was not right. It was then, because of this problematic turn of events and the sense that there must be a better way that he embarked on a search. The search became a journey. The journey led to a series of awakenings. In this journey he discovered several important business thinkers. There was Eliyahu Goldratt who some us know from his book *The Goal*, and who developed the Theory of Constraints. There was Taiichi Ohno who developed the principles of just-in-time manufacturing which became a key component of the Toyota Production System. And there was W. Edwards Deming, the preeminent quality expert, statistician and scientist, who I consider to be my mentor, and who showed me conclusively that Western management was flawed. You will meet many other wise souls here: Lao Tzu, zen masters, neuroscientists and wise workers without major titles to name a few.

But you will not find many of the most quoted business authors, who hold very different views of management. While Bob is not alone in his view of good management it is unfortunate that many business schools and many business authors continue to preach something very different and counter to what you will find in this book. Too often respected, highly quoted business authors obsess on the competition. They suggest treating suppliers at arm's length and with distrust; employees as mere spreadsheet inputs. They advocate pushing for results without understanding or even acknowledging the process. They fail to understand variation. They pay lip service to the customer and put profit ahead of people and process.

Referring to the previous sentence I would like to make one key point. Putting profits first does not lead to great profits. It often leads to the destruction of the company. Putting customers, quality and process first and focusing on those—as long as one has taken the time to master the understanding in this book—will result in much greater profit than anyone thought possible. This is true even in the short run. In the long run it leads to a runaway success for a company. Too many people who claim to understand Deming or quality give the impression that good management is a trade off with profit. That is completely wrong. Bob Browne demonstrated that with a more holistic, systems based, customer focused, variation savvy management understanding, great profitability is not only possible, but probably inevitable.

In his own words, "As we began to realize that it was the caring relationships that allowed the process to become precise, we also became increasingly aware of the significance of variation in everything we do and the need to be open to new and improved paradigms as we let go of old beliefs that had served us so well before." Relationships are the golden thread that hold good management together. Understanding this can be an important catalyst to transformation of one's thinking, feeling and doing.

A second key point is science. In developing his management system Bob was being scientific in the best sense of the word. What is science? A discipline moves from being a discipline, philosophy or religion when the ideas and beliefs begin to interact and be tested by reality. If one is not open to having his old beliefs disproved after testing and use then his ideas form a religion or philosophy, at best. At worst they are but a collection of prejudices. When one conducts a test there needs to be a possible negative outcome that at least indicates the hypothesis being tested is false. Enough of these should lead to a reexamination of the hypothesis and in time the beliefs that underlie it. That is only rational and, in my opinion, a necessary condition to be called scientific.

Yet in management too often the same ideas are repeated endlessly even though the results are poor. One example that affects us all is education. In the US today the Federal Government and others keep pushing for more solutions that make the teacher responsible for his or her results, reward on the basis of one test without having any understanding of variation. Developing teachers, engendering pride and joy in the profession of teaching seems to be off the table. Yet the overall results for our educational system keeps deteriorating. What is the solution of the Federal Government and others? More of the same. More testing, more rewards and punishment. The same management ideas which regularly destroy companies are being used to destroy education in the US.

A third key point would be that even with the success of Great Plains Coca-Cola Bottling under Bob Browne and many other success stories it is still very difficult for many western trained managers to appreciate, understand or believe that this can work so well. And the question is why?

That is a question Bob Browne has been asking himself for many years. In addition to learning how he put together a unique process that drew insights from great management thinkers you, the reader, will learn insights into the depth of change that is necessary and why so many otherwise competent people are unable to accept this kind of management.

I said at the beginning that this book is much more than a how-to book on running a successful company and making an atypical return. As the subtitle of the book suggests, this book represents an emerging leadership philosophy, a combination of Western Logic and Eastern flow. This is a journey to understand. Taiichi Ohno said he really liked the word understand. It implies what lies beneath and holds up and supports the thinking and ideas. It implies the roots. And this book will take you on a journey to understand our roots as a culture and our management style, systems and beliefs.

Rafael Aguayo
Founding Member, Deming Collaboration
July 17, 2014 , Setauket, NY

AUTHOR OF
Dr. Deming: The American Who Taught the Japanese about Quality
The MetaKnowledge Advantage
The Depression of 2016

W.E. Deming is generally recognized by the Japanese as the man most responsible for sparking their economic renaissance starting in 1950. Later, Aguayo and Deming enjoyed a close relationship with weekly face-to-face meetings and a constant exchange of material for more than seven years. As a result his 1990 book, *Dr. Deming: The American Who Taught the Japanese about Quality*, became an instant business best seller. Deming himself called it the best book on his teachings, so far. Tony Robbins called it "the best book I have read on business in a decade," and according to USA Today, it was one of three books former President Bill Clinton said every American should read.

Preface

*T*he master in the art of living makes little distinction between his work and his play, his labor and his leisure, his mind and his body, his education and his recreation, his love and his religion. He hardly knows which is which. He simply pursues his vision of excellence in whatever he does, leaving others to decide whether he is working or playing. To him he is always doing both.

When I began to write the book you are holding, it never occurred to me that this seemingly ancient Zen Buddhist text might apply to me.[1]

I wasn't writing it for the general public. I was writing it for me. I was writing it for the associates of the company I ran for more than 30 years. I was writing it for my family, for my legacy.

It wasn't until I began to write and reflect back that I realized it really was for you, the reader, and for people who realize there is something not quite right with our traditional leadership philosophies . . . for people who would like to experience a better way.

The Coke business has been my life's work. At first I thought I was in it just for me — but looking back I realize I was simply *in it* . . . just like the Zen Buddhist quoted above who left it to others to decide whether he was working or playing.

And, now that I am retired, I see that out of my own journey has emerged a real-life case study — one that, perhaps, points to the resolution of an issue that faces most businesses today.

In the midst of truly revolutionary change:

Why have leadership philosophies changed so little?

Is there a better way?

There are countless examples of the warp-speed change affecting us all: globalization, breakthroughs in science and technology, the explosive growth

---

1 Although this quote is often attributed to an unknown Buddhist monk, it may more accurately be attributed to L. P. Jacks, an early 20th-century English philosopher.

of Big Data, and the increasing diversity and complexity in so many aspects of our lives.

It can be argued that larger and more established organizations have a vested interest in maintaining and sustaining their traditional ways. After all, they have far more to lose and much more to protect.

Maybe this is part of the reason that traditional leadership philosophies are so slow to change, and why cultures so predictably lag behind changes in technology. But, with the ever-increasing pace of change that lies ahead of us, this presents an obvious problem.

To the extent that these larger establishments do not evolve quickly, this can create a competitive advantage for the smaller, more nimble, and more entrepreneurial organizations. Said another way, organizations that transform their traditional leadership philosophies can become a disruptive threat to those who sustain their traditional ways.

And . . . of course, on a personal level, this could also apply to you and to me. Let's be honest: most of us human beings, too, are slow to change our mental models and to modify our entrenched habits — partly because of the culture of the organizations we inhabit.

That is what this book is all about. It is about transforming traditional leadership philosophies into something that in many ways is very different; yet in other ways, it simply complements what we have always done so well. But in all ways, it is much more relevant to where we are today — as well as to what lies ahead. It affects the way we think, our habits, and the culture of our organizations. I will refer to this emerging leadership philosophy as "Sys-Tao."

Changing your mind is hard.

Changing your habits is harder.

**Changing an organization's culture
is even more difficult.**

The "Sys" in *Sys-Tao* represents our traditional western ways of thinking, while the "Tao" is symbolic of methods rooted in the eastern traditions. Sys-Tao is therefore an amalgamation, a synthesis, of two worldviews that will allow us to better thrive in the world we all inhabit.

The works of W. Edwards Deming, the American who taught the Japanese about quality, heavily influenced *Sys-Tao*. In his own words, he also captures what this book is about. We must:

> Adopt the new philosophy. We are in a new economic age.
> Western management must awaken to the challenge, must learn
> their responsibilities, and take on leadership for change.

Despite his influence in Japan, Deming really never caught on in our western culture, and he has had little effect on our traditional leadership philosophies. Nevertheless, modern-day social science and neuroscience theories are slowly discovering what he was saying more than sixty years before.

Deming, of course, lacked the science, but he provided the map. We have just been slow to understand. This book is based on his map, my experience, and more current explanations from other thinkers. In the spirit of collaboration, many of these thinkers are referenced along the way, and they are also linked to the book's website, Sys-Tao.org, which in turn will link you to their Internet sites.

If you are reading this on an e-book or other device with Internet capability, just click on the hyperlinks in the text. To get back to the book, just close your browser. Otherwise, if you are reading a printed version, just go to our website, Sys-Tao.org, and you can easily find the resource you are looking for on the links page.

The Sys-Tao philosophy is mostly the result of 20 years of experience-based changes to our operating systems and processes that was preceded by a period of what I call traditional leadership philosophies. It is difficult to say which came first: the principles we refer to as our new leadership philosophy, or the processes that make up our improved operating systems. They emerged together.

> **Tao is a principle. Creation, on the other hand, is a process.**
> **That is all there is; principle and process, how and what.**
> ~ **Lao Tzu's** *Tao Te Ching*

Sys-Tao, as you will see, is code for these principles and processes, and it is applicable to any business. It just so happens that our business was Coca-Cola.

The Coke business makes a great case study for traditional leadership philosophies because few businesses have been around longer than Coca-Cola, and the Coke business is easy to understand — everyone can relate to an ice-cold Coke.

I, too, have been around a long time. I was a "third-generation bottler" — my career with Coke spans more than 40 years, and I was the chairman and CEO of Great Plains Coca-Cola Bottling Company for more than 30 years. That makes me an expert in this very traditional business.

In 1922, my grandfather purchased what was to become Great Plains Coca-Cola Bottling Company. He ran the company for about 30 years until he handed over the reins to my father, who was also in charge for nearly 30 years. In 1980, my brother and I engineered a leveraged buy-out and bought the company, and so it became my turn to run Great Plains.

Then, as I pondered my own retirement, our associates roasted me on April Fool's Day, 2010 — 30 years to the day after we'd purchased the company. They gave me a 12-pack of Coke with an appropriate adaptation of the lyrics of one of Tim McGraw's country songs there beside my photo and our iconic logo:

The ending of an era and the turning of a page
Now it's time to focus in on where we go from here
Lord, have mercy on our next 30 years.

In our next 30 years, we're going to have some fun,
Try to forget about all the crazy things we've done.
We'll do it better in our next 30 years,
We'll cry a little less; laugh a little more.
Figure out what we're doing here in our next 30 years.

Our next 30 years will be the best ones of our life.
Spending precious moments
With the ones that we hold dear;
Making up for lost time, in our next 30 years.

That's when I decided to write this book, but I quickly realized that this story is not about our proud past, our accomplishments, or me. It is about the journey that we took together.

At first, we didn't even realize we were on a journey. Yet somewhere along the way we had changed our minds — our leadership philosophy; we had changed our habits — our operating methods; and, most importantly, we had changed our culture — from a command and control structure to a more lifelike process control environment. Our aim now was simply "to become better." Numerical goals as we had come to know them became less important, yet we were making more money, and having more fun.

I also realized that there was an additional purpose for this book: This transformation was disruptive by traditional standards — even though our customers appreciated it, even though our associates were more joyful, and even though the value of our business appreciated because of it — very few of our peers in the industry could understand it. They respected it because it worked, but they did not believe it could be replicated . . . but it can!

> **In the end, people are persuaded not by what we say,**
> **but by what they understand.**
>
> **~ John C. Maxwell**

It is my hope that this book will help them, and you, understand.

We were able to "understand," not because we were unique, but because our associates embraced these principles and made these processes real. Everyone wants to become better, and the transformation was everybody's job. We did it together, and so can you.

It is significant that on December 30, 2011, we sold Great Plains to The Coca-Cola Company. We had grown to become the fifth largest bottler of Coca-Cola in North America, and we were recognized as being world-class in our industry. We had just completed the most successful year in our company's history. We had clearly become better. But on that day we ended a 90-year Browne family tradition, while promising a new beginning with The Coca-Cola Company for the associates of the Great Plains Coca-Cola Family.

Whether these principles and processes will be integrated with the more traditional leadership philosophies of The Coca-Cola Company might someday make another case study. So, the additional purpose of this book is to explain why so many successful organizations and so many smart people have difficulty appreciating these ideas while other emerging entities seem to accept them so easily.

PART ONE

Background

*T*he soft drink industry was quite literally born in drug stores in the South during the reconstruction years following the Civil War. Its history is well documented via links at the Sys-Tao website (Sys-Tao.org/links).

CHAPTER ONE

The Soft Drink Industry and Coca-Cola

My grandfather, Virgil Browne, was born in 1878 in Mt. Pleasant, Texas. He lived to be 102 years old and died just before midnight New Year's Eve, 1979. Had he lived just 30 minutes longer, he would have lived in 12 decades. I was 36 years old when he died and had numerous opportunities to hear him recount those early years.

According to him, the Southern economy was decimated by the war and the freedom of the slaves. His mother had died at an early age, and his father, Spill, instilled in him the need to be entrepreneurial and self-reliant. One story has it that young Virgil and his brother, Will, spent an entire summer with their father traveling all over east Texas on a buckboard wagon trying to sell wash tubs and scrub boards with an attached clothes wringer to the settlers in the area. The origin of this entrepreneurial scheme came from what he referred to as "Yankee peddlers from back east." He said, "Some people referred to them as carpetbaggers." The Yankee peddlers were the supply chain and the Brownes were the distributors. According to Granddad, they washed clothes for every settler in six counties, but never sold a single washboard.

Later, about 1900, he began working as a "soda jerk" in one of the two drug stores in Mt. Pleasant, Texas. He would tell us stories of what it was like when the cowboys would ride through town shooting their pistols into the air in celebration after a successful day of driving cattle. He would stand in the street in entrepreneurial fashion waving them down and pointing them to his store in order to drum up business.

One of Virgil's favorite stories was about a time when one of the peddlers came through Mt. Pleasant on a day that the storeowner was out of town. Young Virgil took it upon himself to go ahead and place an order with the peddler, without any authority to do so. He bought some railroad pocket watches and ladies' handkerchiefs, among other things. When the storeowner arrived back in town a few days later, he was furious at Virgil's actions.

Nevertheless, those watches and handkerchiefs "sold like hotcakes" and the next time a peddler came to town, Virgil was instructed to go down and make the order. Afterwards, Granddad would often say, "The only thing you can steal and get away with it is responsibility."

In fact, he was really explaining the importance of *quality consciousness* and solving customer problems. He always wondered why people were so often afraid to take responsibility. I don't think he ever realized how traditional leadership philosophies were causing this "fear," or how they would make it increasingly difficult to take responsibility as organizations were to become bigger and more complex over the next 100 years.

In addition to this entrepreneurial spirit, he would tell us the key to running a successful drug store in those days was to be able to sell things that no one else could get. He never said things like "competitive advantage" or "supply chain," but he did explain the importance of the Yankee peddler and taking care of customers.

The peddlers came through town just a few times each year, and their wagons carried very little inventory, but they sold fragrances, perfumes, concentrates, spices and small sundry items that the early day druggists could use to concoct goods their customers would value. For instance, they made soap formed into cakes and scented with the perfumes and fragrances that the peddlers sold. In a similar way, Virgil later concocted Orange Squeeze, a soda drink which opened lots of doors for him to become an early day Coca-Cola bottler.

On May 8, 1886, seventeen years before Granddad created Orange Squeeze, another druggist in Atlanta, Georgia, John Stith Pemberton, concocted his own secret formula. It was at first intended to be a headache remedy that "Relieves Fatigue," but when accidentally mixed with soda water, it turned out to be "Delicious and Refreshing," and was named Coca-Cola. Five years later he sold his secret formula to Asa G. Candler for $2,300.

Then, in 1894, a candy store owner, Joseph A. Biedenharn, installed bottling equipment in the back of his Vicksburg, Mississippi store and began selling Coca-Cola in bottles, up and down the Mississippi River.

Although Biedenharn was the first official Coca-Cola bottler, it was two attorneys from Chattanooga, Tennessee, Benjamin F. Thomas and Joseph P. Whitehead, who created the Coca-Cola "franchised" bottler system. In 1899, they paid just $1.00 for the rights to franchise Coca-Cola nationwide (excluding Vicksburg). The Bottlers were then given the exclusive rights to bottle and sell Coca-Cola in a fixed geographical territory in perpetuity. The Coca-Cola

Company would supply the syrup at a fixed price, and of course, Thomas and Whitehead would collect a royalty.

In 1907, Granddad formed the Parker Browne Company and began selling his Squeeze Flavors to those early day Coca-Cola Bottlers. It was during this time that he became acquainted with Joseph Biedenharn's brother, Ollie. In 1912, they purchased the Texarkana, Arkansas Coca-Cola territory.

In 1916, he joined with another investor, Ira B. Harkey, to form his own franchise company, "The National Fruit Flavor Company," for Squeeze flavors. That same year, with yet another partner, Sam McDaniel, he bought the Ardmore, Oklahoma Coca-Cola territory. Then, in 1922, he joined forces with Harkey and McDaniel to buy the Oklahoma City Coca-Cola territory. They paid $150,000. The Browne interest was $\frac{5}{12}$'s of the deal.

By 1909 there were nearly 400 Coca-Cola Bottlers, and by the 1920s there were over 1,000 bottlers of Coca-Cola. And so, the soft drink industry and Coca-Cola began to grow. But it was not until the 1950s that bottlers sold Coke in anything other than the 6½ ounce returnable bottle. It was not until the 1960s that The Coca-Cola Company offered anything other than the single brand, Coca-Cola.

In a 1963 speech, Crawford Rainwater, one of the more prominent bottlers of Coca-Cola, lamented over this growing complexity brought on by the preceding few years: "One of our plants has gone from one product, packaged in only two ways, to the staggering total of 26 products and packages!"

In the old days the trucks were loaded each day with a standard load from inventory produced the day before, and the route salesmen would make their daily rounds replenishing the inventory for the customers on their route. Clearly, adding 25 stock keeping units (SKUs) added complexity to production, truck loading, selling, order taking, and merchandising.

The aftermath of WWII paved the way for unprecedented growth for the entire US economy. Manufacturers, their customers and their suppliers were all consolidating. Everything was getting bigger. The focus was shifting from Main Street to Wall Street, but the past paradigms, for the most part, did not change. Terms like "economies of scale" were used to explain the need for consolidation, but other than that the business practices of the time could be described as "paving over cow paths." New technologies came along, but typically they were used to automate what people were already doing. Traditional leadership philosophies changed very little.

It had taken more than three fourths of a century for The Coca-Cola Company to reach 26 SKUs. Since that time the number of stock keeping units bottlers sell has climbed to more than 500. In this same period of time, the number of Coca-Cola bottlers in the United States consolidated from over 1000 to less than 70. Fewer than 20 of these actually bottle Coca-Cola today, and the five largest represent over 95% of that total volume.

Modern day orders are "pre-sold," and delivered one to two days later from over 500 distribution centers where inventory is held based on forecasts of what was expected to be needed a week or two before. Furthermore, "economies of scale" increased batch sizes, lengthened cycle times, and disrupted the "just in time" rhythms of the past.

Something is terribly wrong with this picture. We are selling more SKUs, but we are doing it more slowly and not nearly as well. "Out of stock" and "out of date" are industry terms used today, that were unheard of in my grandfather's day. As the pace of change quickened, the issues only became more complex, and our traditional ways were no longer keeping pace.

It is as if the entrepreneurial spirit to serve customers gave way to a goal of simply making more money and getting bigger. There was little concern about getting better, and nearly all U.S. manufacturers were losing ground when it came to world-class comparisons. Specifically, a mysterious eastern culture, that lagged so far behind us just a generation before, was starting to pass us by.

On June 24, 1980, (just a few weeks after we bought Great Plains) an NBC television documentary recognized this American dilemma when it posed the question, "If Japan can . . . why can't we?" This show is credited for beginning the Quality Revolution and introducing the methods of W. Edwards Deming to America. Suddenly, it became evident that in our quest to become bigger we had lost our way to becoming better.

So what did we at Great Plains do? The short answer is nothing. Like most American businesses, we were pretty much oblivious to this new fad that had been bubbling up from Japan for over 30 years. We had no ears for it.

I was well schooled in the American way of doing things, and we still had opportunities to get bigger via consolidations. So what did we do? A slightly longer answer is that we simply accelerated what we had already been doing. We "recycled ignorance," to use one of Deming's favorite expressions.

We took on more debt and bought more neighboring bottlers and got bigger. We doubled our size, but we did not become better. It took nearly ten years for us to realize there really was something to that 1980 TV show.

Unfortunately, for most of us this cultural gap continued to grow, because most American businesses never really ever understood the so-called Quality

Revolution. As a result, the *"quality"* movement stalled for most Americans, but somehow, ten years later, Great Plains was transformed.

But these three questions remain unanswered: If Japan could . . . why couldn't we? If Great Plains did, . . . why don't others? Why is it that the traditional leadership philosophies within our established organizations have changed so little?

It will be my job to answer these questions for you and, of course, I will also explain how we did it.

CHAPTER TWO

Great Plains Coca-Cola Bottling Company

I t is often said, "out of crisis comes order." Deming's most famous book was in fact titled, *Out of the Crisis*. He wrote it in 1982 as a result of the Quality Revolution that he had started in Japan more than 30 years before.

At the time, I was completely unaware of Deming and of the crisis he was writing about. Instead I was, as I saw myself then, thirty-nine years old, well educated, smart, on top of my game and invincible. I had just pulled off what the American Dream was all about. I had bought the family business, and all I had to do now was put the accelerator down and take off — the sky was my limit.

It was my intent to seize this opportunity, to act quickly, to take market share from Pepsi, to pay down our debt, and claim success.

This of course would require strategic change. There was nothing subtle about our approach. By 1988 we had completed a series of acquisitions that nearly doubled the size of our company, and it was time to follow up with the necessary reorganizing, restructuring, and reengineering of the entire company.

We employed the familiar western approach to the situation at hand. We performed a strategic assessment of the competitive landscape. For instance: Strengths, Weaknesses, Opportunities, and Threats (SWOT) were analyzed to determine a master plan for change.

It seemed obvious that with the increased debt and the increased size of the company, it was time to achieve our own "economies of scale" and streamline the operations.

Systems Thinking was something I thought I understood, and soon we had flow charts of all sorts of things showing boxes with arrows connecting other boxes, sprinkled in with triangles that represented decision points — if yes then . . . if no then . . . It was so well thought out, predetermined, and precise — no room for guesswork. We had clear-cut goals and objectives, and a strategy to win.

Our vision was to make everything and everyone more efficient. We wanted to reduce head count and incentivize success. There were "no sacred cows;" everything was focused on what was best for the company.

We made progress — two steps forward, then one step back. We learned a lot — mostly the hard way — but there was always a lurking feeling that we were doing something wrong. *There must be a better way.* I began questioning our traditional leadership philosophies, I began reading books, and I even attended a few seminars.

But we were getting results, even if they were forced changes. I reasoned that if it weren't for our well-developed system of incentive plans — carrots, sticks, and the veiled threats from most of us that "it was our way or the highway" — we probably would have accomplished very little. No one seemed to be accepting the changes we were implementing. But, we were getting some "good" results, and for us, at that time, that was all that mattered.

Little did I realize that I was creating my own crisis.

Then it happened. In 1993 I was introduced to the Teamsters Union. The unrest we had created was a welcome sign for them and a crisis for me. For more than two years they tried to unionize our company, and in 1998 they tried again. They were not successful, and I give the Teamsters no credit. They brought no solutions. They only tried to exploit the situation. The acquisitions didn't create the crisis. I did it by myself. I really did believe we were doing the right things, but instead we had created a crisis by doing those things I had been trained so well to do. Our way out of that crisis represents a transformation in our leadership philosophies — not unlike the one Deming had written about.

Throughout the decade of the 90s, we learned the hard way what Deming had been trying to tell us for more than forty years.

PART TWO

Conceptual Foundations

*T*he intuitive mind is a sacred gift, and
the rational mind is a faithful servant.
We have created a society that honors
the servant and has forgotten the gift.

~ Albert Einstein

CHAPTER THREE

Profound Knowledge

W. EDWARDS DEMING

As I set out to introduce the conceptual material that underpins this book, it seems appropriate to begin in the same way it all began for me: with the works of W. Edwards Deming. Dr. Deming (1900–1993) is generally recognized as the father of Total Quality Management, abbreviated as TQM. He is often referred to as the American who taught the Japanese about quality, because that is where the movement began after WWII.

When Japanese manufacturers applied his methods, they experienced unheard-of levels of quality and productivity. This, combined with the lower costs that resulted, created international demand for Japanese products. Despite being considered something of a hero in Japan, he was only just beginning to win widespread recognition in the U.S. at the time of his death. His accomplishments are well documented in a three-part video series at Sys-Tao.org/links.

Deming was a statistician. He was not an accountant. He was not a particularly good communicator and he wrote very little until he was 80 years old. As a result, his choice of words and metaphors often made him sound old-fashioned and outdated. For instance, during his lectures he would refer to his overhead projector as a "lantern." Today, even overhead projectors are outdated.

Furthermore, he was writing about a very different paradigm, one that is foreign to our western culture and our traditional leadership philosophies. For example, his *Statistical Process Control* (SPC) concepts deal with the "variations" more than the "averages," something that comes naturally to eastern cultures that are more accustomed to the yin and yang of our world. By contrast, most Westerners are more linear and analytical in their thinking. We eschew ambiguities and tend to just settle in on the average as the number that matters most.

In everything from quarterly earnings to batting averages, we feel more comfortable distilling data down into one representative number that measures the results vs. the goal. The Japanese, on the other hand, are likely to be more interested in the variations in these outcomes, in the consistency of the aim of the process that delivered these results.

Maybe that is partly why the Japanese so readily adapted to his thinking and we did not.

Deming organized his thinking into four broad categories that are difficult to comprehend separately because they are so interdependent. When taken holistically, these four topics represent what he called *The System of Profound Knowledge*:

- **Understanding Psychology**
- **Systems Thinking**
- **Understanding Variation**
- **The Theory of Knowledge**

To make understanding Deming even more difficult, he had Fourteen Points, five of which (3, 4, 10, 11, and 12) go for the jugular of some of our traditional western leadership philosophies. And the other nine points seem so simplistic that their meaning is lost without careful study:

1. **Create constancy of purpose toward improvement of product and service, with the aim to become competitive and stay in business, and to provide jobs.**

2. **Adopt the new philosophy. We are in a new economic age. Western management must awaken to the challenge, must learn their responsibilities, and take on leadership for change.**

3. **Cease dependence on inspection to achieve quality. Eliminate the need for massive inspection by building quality into the product in the first place.**

4. **End the practice of awarding business on the basis of price tag. Instead, minimize total cost. Move towards a single supplier for any one item, on a long-term relationship of loyalty and trust.**

5. **Improve constantly and forever the system of production and service, to improve quality and productivity, and thus constantly decrease costs.**

6. **Institute training on the job.**

7. **Institute leadership. The aim of supervision should be to help people, machines, and gadgets to do a better job. Supervision of management is in need of overhaul, as well as supervision of production workers.**

8. **Drive out fear, so that everyone may work effectively for the company.**

9. **Break down barriers between departments. People in research, design, sales, and production must work as a team, to foresee problems of production and in use that may be encountered with the product or service.**

10. **Eliminate slogans, exhortations, and targets for the work force asking for zero defects and new levels of productivity. Such exhortations only create adversarial relationships, as the bulk of the causes of low quality and low productivity belong to the system and thus lie beyond the power of the work force.**

11. a. **Eliminate work standards (quotas) on the factory floor. Substitute leadership.**

    b. **Eliminate management by objective. Eliminate management by numbers, numerical goals. Substitute leadership.**

12. a. **Remove barriers that rob the hourly worker of his right to pride of workmanship. The responsibility of supervisors must be changed from sheer numbers to quality.**

    b. **Remove barriers that rob people in management and in engineering of their right to pride of workmanship. This means, "inter alia, abolishment of the annual or merit rating and of management by objective."**

13. **Institute a vigorous program of education and self-improvement.**

14. **Put everybody in the company to work to accomplish the transformation. The transformation is everybody's job.**

Furthermore, in 1984, he also listed "Five Deadly Diseases" affecting western management. You can see this video and more of *The Wisdom of Deming* at Sys-Tao.org/links.

Nevertheless, it is no wonder that most people don't know much about this man. With a quick look, it is not surprising that most people don't care. For most of us, our traditional leadership philosophies make perfect sense, and this all sounds like gibberish. But he was deliberate and thoughtful in organizing these ideas, and careful study of them is rewarded with cues toward a very different — and perhaps better — way of leadership.

Because his ideas are for the most part so counterintuitive to our culture, it is my opinion that it takes "just-like" references and metaphors to comprehend what he was saying. For example, let's delve more deeply into his distinction between "goals" and "aims." We think of "goals" as being very positive things. We set goals, we work toward them, and we hope to achieve them. That's all very common in our western ways. But Deming didn't like the word — to him it was something of a pejorative. "Goals" are numerical standards that have binary metrics — they're either met, or they aren't. Instead of "goal," he used "aim." The distinction may seem subtle, or even needlessly picky, but it's worth exploring.

Since the word "goal," for us, conjures sports, let's use that as a "just-like" reference. In American football, we have field goals, worth three points for each successful score. This is right along the lines of most western thinking: it's binary; it's easy to define; the ball is kicked and it either goes between the posts or it doesn't. It's either in, or it's out.

But what if the Japanese had designed the field goal? Instead of the western version on the left, their adaptation might look like the one shown on the right:

In American football it is *acceptable* to hit the upright and bounce in for a three-point field goal. In my hypothetical Japanese version, the *aim* is to be right down the middle. It is most *desirable* and worth three points, but as the ball moves to the right or left, the result would become worth less and less, and it would then become negative as it diverged beyond the specification limits set by our traditional upright standards.

In this alternative version of our game, the emphasis has shifted from "good enough to achieve a goal" to the notion of continual improvement of a process.

Well, needless, to say, this rule change is way more than the typical American football fan can deal with, and yet this is just one example of the many distinctions we can draw from Deming's teachings. Furthermore, his teachings must be taken together as an interdependent whole if they are to be fully appreciated.

But one thing is clear: something really is terribly wrong with our western ways, and Japan, China, South Korea, and even India all seem to be passing us by.

It is as if our western civilization has created cultural blind spots that keep most westerners from appreciating what Deming was trying to teach us — something that the Japanese and other Asian cultures seem to understand naturally.

In a serendipitous way, it occurred to me that these cultural blind spots might be rooted in what can be termed "left vs. right" brained thinking.

> The left side of our brain is more narrowly focused on what we already know is important and what requires greater attention to discrete details. It is a closed system with a simplified view of reality. On the other hand, the right side of our brain is more broadly vigilant, and open to relationships and uncertainties in an interconnected world that is alive, inclusive, constantly evolving, and always changing.

This quote is from Iain McGilchrist's 2009 book, *The Master and His Emissary: The Divided Brain and the Making of the Western World*. It should be noted that McGilchrist is not referring to *what* is happening in each hemisphere; he is referring to *how* each hemisphere processes the same information differently. (See *The Divided Brain* at Sys-Tao.org/links).

Serendipity, Asian cultures, left- vs. right-brained thinking, and Deming himself are all hard for western minds to comprehend, so let's take it one step at a time. First, I'll approach this "left- vs. right-sided" thinking hypothesis in a more linear and anecdotal way. But remember, in the final analysis everything is interdependent and it must be taken holistically.

CHAPTER FOUR

Cultural Roots — West Meets East

One anecdotal way to explain these cultural blind spots, and how they might be rooted in the differences in "left- vs. right-brained" thinking, is for me to show you what my own Anglo-Saxon ancestry looks like as far back as my Browne family lineage is documented.

There are six known generations of Brownes that precede me, and without exception, there was a steady progression away from dependence on others and towards independence, self-reliance, rugged individualism, entrepreneurism, and the Manifest Destiny of the American Dream. These left-brained values sustained us for all of these six generations.

Nowhere in this progression, in my family or in American history, is there much evidence of movement towards interdependence and tolerance for others. For instance, the Trail of Tears moved the Indians west to Indian Territory (what later became Oklahoma), in order to make room for the white settlers from the east. Although we later let them assimilate into our culture, we never assimilated much of their culture into ours. Likewise, we fought a civil war over slavery, but did little regarding civil rights for over 100 years. Even women's rights were slow to evolve throughout most of this time.

Looked at this way, "We the people" was a fairly exclusive group of left-brained thinkers, and not until recently — generation seven on this timeline — did these "winner take all" attitudes begin to fail us, and open the way for more inclusive right-brained thinking.

BROWNE FAMILY LINEAGE

❶ Daniel Browne, born 1755 in Virginia Commonwealth

In the era preceding the Declaration of Independence, and the beginning of the end of our dependence as a colony, he was a Baptist Preacher who revolted against the Church of England and the unpopular tobacco taxes. He migrated to Kentucky to avoid persecution and to remain independent.

② George Pemberton Browne, born (c.1775) in Kentucky

In the era of Daniel Boone, he was an early day independent agrarian settler in the preindustrial United States.

③ John Tanner Browne, born 1815 in Kentucky

In the era of Horace Greely — "Go west young man, go west" — he migrated to Alabama circa 1830. It was also the era of Manifest Destiny, the belief that it was God's will for the American people to expand their territory and governance across the North American continent. Ironically, he followed the same route as the Trail of Tears that was moving the Indians west to Oklahoma at that same time.

④ Spillman Browne, born 1855 in Alabama

In the era of the American Cowboy and the cattle drives (1865 – 1885), he continued the pioneer migration to Texas. It was also the era of Reconstruction in the South (1865 – 1877) following the Civil War. The southern economy was in disarray as a result of the war and the end of slavery, but the entrepreneurial spirit thrived.

⑤ Virgil Browne, born 1877 in Mount Pleasant, Texas

It was the era of Horatio Alger's rags-to-riches men. After several entrepreneurial ventures in Texas and Louisiana, he moved to Oklahoma City, Oklahoma in 1922 to pioneer one of the early day Coca-Cola bottling companies. It can be said that the soft drink industry was born in drug stores across the south during this era:

- 1885 Dr Pepper invented by a pharmacist in Waco, Texas
- 1886 Coca-Cola invented by a pharmacist in Atlanta, Georgia
- 1898 Pepsi-Cola invented by a pharmacist in New Caleb, North Carolina
- 1903 Virgil Browne, a pharmacist, invents Squeeze Orange Soda in Ft. Worth, Texas

⑥ Henry Browne, born 1906 in Ft. Worth, Texas

It was in this era, following WWII, when the U.S. economy first dominated the world economy and when Coca-Cola became the first truly global brand name. It was the generation Tom Brokaw referred to as "The Greatest Generation." My dad moved to Oklahoma in 1922 with his father and later ran The Oklahoma Coca-Cola Bottling Company for the 30 years prior to 1980.

⑦ Robert Browne, born 1943 in Oklahoma City, Oklahoma

In this era of the Baby Boomers, everything peaked for our American Way. Slowly, though, things did change. Wars since WWII have been less popular; our U.S. economy has become less dominant and for the first time in six generations, independence has given way to the beginning of a new era of global interdependence, sustainability, and tolerance. For the first time in all these generations, "We the people," really has begun to include all of us. It is as if the more right-brained mindset of the Asian cultures is somehow becoming more relevant. It was during this era — from 1980 until 2012 — that I had the good fortune to run the company my dad and granddad had built.

⑧ William E. Browne, born in 1978 in Oklahoma City, Oklahoma

Web, as we call him, was born with a heart condition that resulted in a stroke on the left side of his brain. Today, he is a well-adjusted, college-educated adult with a wife, a daughter, and a son (generation 9) of his own, but he is clearly a right-brained personality. Web's situation created the serendipity that caused me to first become interested in the differences in left- vs. right-brained personalities.

It was not until I saw two movies, *Lonesome Dove* (1989) and *Dances with Wolves* (1990) that it occurred to me there could be such a thing as left- or right-brained *cultures*.

The Academy Award-winning picture of the year, *Dances with Wolves*, starring Kevin Costner, depicts the plight of the American Indians about ten years before my grandfather was born. Specifically, a Civil War hero, Lt. Dunbar, finds himself alone in a wilderness territory occupied by Sioux Indians and separated from his military past. Slowly, Dunbar's predisposed blind spot regarding the more right-brained Indian culture begins to fade:

> Nothing I have been told about these people is correct. They are
> not thieves or beggars. They are not the boogeymen they are made
> out to be. On the contrary, they are polite guests and I enjoy their
> humor. They were a people so eager to laugh, so devoted to family, so
> dedicated to each other. The only word that comes to mind is harmony.
> It was hard to know how to feel. I had never been in a battle like this
> one. This had not been a fight for territory or riches or to make men
> free. This battle had no ego. It had been fought to preserve the food
> stores that would see us (them) through winter, to protect the lives of
> women and children and loved ones only a few feet away. I felt a pride
> I had never felt before. The efficiency of the people, and the speed at
> which they move, was enough to impress any military commander.

I can imagine that my great-grandfather — "Spill," as they called him — probably didn't have any sense of this sentiment as he made his journey west into Texas. The American culture of the time just did not have eyes or ears for the alternative culture it had displaced, and the movie drives this point home. It's significant that Costner's character doesn't come to appreciate the beauty of the "boogeymen" until he's completely isolated from his own culture. Only then, once he's out of the shadow of the things he's been told, can he see that it was a blind spot all along.

On the other hand, *Lonesome Dove*, starring Robert Duvall, depicts the era of the cattle drives. Specifically, it is set in 1876, the very year before my grandfather was born. The shift, from agrarian slave owners with zero tolerance for the American Indians, towards the gilded age of the Industrial Revolution and the belief in the Manifest Destiny of the American Way, is captured in this exchange from *Lonesome Dove*:

> **Woodrow**: [*riding into San Antonio*] Things sure have changed
> since the last time I was here. It's all growed up.

Gus: Of course it's growed up, Woodrow. We killed all the Indians and bandits so the bankers could move in.

Woodrow: Only a fool would want the Indians back.

Gus: Has it ever occurred to you, Woodrow; that all the work we done were for the bankers? Hell, we killed off everybody made this country interestin'!

These men, unlike Lt. Dunbar in the last example, are still fully entrenched in their own culturally based prejudice. However, despite this, one of them has a sense that something isn't quite right with the "progress" of this westward expansion. He hints at a feeling, however shrouded it may be, that the work they've been doing has only served the "bankers" — whose goal is to make money — and that maybe along the way, in ridding the place of this disparate culture, they had actually lost something more valuable.

In yet another example, it is what's left out that speaks volumes regarding these cultural blind spots. A source of state pride for all of us Oklahomans is the stage play *Oklahoma!* It was the longest-running Broadway production of all time. It began its run in 1943, the year I was born. The setting was in 1906 in Indian Territory, the year before Oklahoma was to become a state, and the year my father was born. The word itself, "Oklahoma," is derived from the Choctaw words meaning "red people." But, ironically, there is not a single Indian character. One of the play's famous songs is even titled, "The Farmer and the Cowman Should be Friends," but there is not one reference to the "Cowboys and the Indians."

And so, in a serendipitous way, it occurred to me that while my culturally left-brained ancestors headed west, and while their intolerance for the more culturally right-brained Indians grew, the blind spots that resulted might be part of the reason that Americans have so much difficulty understanding what Deming had to say and why the more right-brained Asian cultures found it so easy to embrace.

Biologically, of course, we are all more alike than different. However, it seems self-evident that our cultural bias can in some ways be attributed to the way we, as a culture, choose to use our brains.

Some of the cultural distinctions that derive from the differences in the way we think are summarized below under my own metaphorical heading . . . Cowboys and Indians:

Some Cultural Distinctions

COWBOYS		INDIANS
left-brained	≈	right-brained
linear, logical, *what*	≈	cyclical analogical, *how*
cause & effect dependencies	≈	collaborative interdependencies
precise systems	≈	caring relationships
win/lose competition	≈	win/win cooperation
pragmatic & analytical	≈	relationships in need of feedback
accomplishing goals	≈	solving problems
functional, hierarchical structures	≈	holistic networking communities
radical change	≈	continual improvement
training to change others	≈	learning for self-improvement
extrinsic motives	≈	intrinsic values
ownership	≈	stewardship
manipulative	≈	appreciative
acceptability	≈	desirability
managing people for objectives	≈	managing processes for improvement
Reality is in the Results	≈	*Reality is in the Process*

When you relax, slow down, and allow yourself to more empathically consider these right-brained cultural distinctions, it becomes easier to understand why the Japanese could more easily comprehend what Deming was telling us.

There has been a great deal written regarding the distinctions between the oriental cultures of the east vs. occidental ways of the west. The consensus among these texts is that the one is highly intuitive, while the other is mostly rational. While neither is inherently *better* than the other, if we cannot appreciate both, then surely some part of our understanding will be lost.

These distinctions are not about *what* goes on in one hemisphere as opposed to the other. Instead, these distinctions deal with *how* these two sides of our brains process the same information in different ways. According to Albert Einstein:

> *The intuitive mind is a sacred gift, and*
> *the rational mind is a faithful servant.*
> *We have created a society that honors*
> *the servant and has forgotten the gift.*

It is as if our left hemisphere is unaware (blind) of its need for the right, while the right side understands its need for the left but has difficulty expressing it.

Whether these cultural distinctions are actually the result of a right-brained vs. left-brained preference is, of course, debatable. Dr. Richard E. Nisbett addresses this debate in his 2003 book, *The Geography of Thought: How Asians and Westerners Think Differently . . . and Why*. According to Nisbett, people who grow up in different cultures do not just think about different things: they think differently. **Appendix I** contains a *New York Times* article that summarizes his thesis in greater detail. The thesis is further complemented in a video, *West and East, Cultural Differences*, at Sys-Tao.org/links.

It is my opinion that these cultural distinctions, that take root in how we have historically chosen to use the most reflective parts of our brains, create perceptions that in turn affect and underpin our beliefs about the world we live in.

These beliefs affect our actions, and as our actions become common practice, they become habits. In this way, our deep-seated ways of thinking become rooted in our habits.

Consider for a moment the example of a grandmaster chess player. The future grandmaster probably begins playing chess at a very young age, as many kids do. And because he shows promise, his parents start him on chess lessons. As he improves, he starts playing tournaments and hanging around chess clubs after school. He immerses himself in a culture of chess.

The more he plays, the faster and better he's able to analyze a chessboard. He is able to recognize complicated patterns that you or I would never see, and he can do it fast. In this way, the reflective thinking he's done in his studies becomes more and more reflexive — it becomes habit. Soon, he can beat average players without even really thinking much, because to him the moves and patterns of the board are automatic.

But it doesn't stop there. Before long, he starts to see "just-like" references to chess in every aspect of his life. All of his problem-solving ability is rooted in the idea of moves and counter-moves. It's Maslow's Law of the Instrument in action — "to a man with only a hammer, everything looks like a nail."

This is an exaggerated example of what happens to all of us, and to our brains. We are all immersed in our own cultures and our own perceptions of reality. We are influenced by these patterns and values, in ways that eventually come to define the way we think — they define the way that our brain "selects in" information that is meaningful to our current paradigm and filters out what seems extraneous to our interests. You may not be a chess master, but I'll bet you perform some pretty complicated tasks in your daily life, almost without thinking. How many times have you driven home from the grocery store, only to realize you were operating on "autopilot" the whole time?

Aristotle said it more concisely: "We are what we repeatedly do; excellence then, is not an act, but a habit." Said still another way, "Practice makes perfect," but then, only if you are practicing the right thing! A more accurate statement might be, "Practice makes permanent."

Habits require very little conscious thought. They are triggered by our limbic system, and what is often called our "reptilian brain." These are the most primitive, least thoughtful, most reflexive, least flexible, and fastest-reacting parts of our brain. It is no wonder that it is so difficult to embrace cultural distinctions that seem so foreign to us. This little poem from an anonymous source says it pretty well:

> I am your constant companion.
> I am your greatest helper or your heaviest burden.
> I will push you onward or drag you down to failure.
> I am completely at your command.
> Half the things you do, you might just as well turn over to me
> and I will be able to do them quickly and correctly.
> I am easily managed; you must merely be firm with me.
> Show me exactly how you want something done,
> and after a few lessons I will do it automatically.
> I am the servant of all great men, and alas, of all failures as well.
> Those who are great, I have made them great.
> Those who are failures, I have made failures.
> I am not a machine though I work with the precision of a machine,
> plus the intelligence of man.
> You may run me for profit, or run me for ruin;
> it makes no difference to me.
> Take me, train me, be firm with me,
> and I will put the world at your feet.
> Be easy with me and I will destroy you.
> Who am I? I am Habit.

For these reasons, just understanding and appreciating "right-brained" distinctions like those listed above is not enough. One must also internalize these new ideas by modifying old habits and creating new habits. Finally, and most importantly, your cultural environment must accept your new habits. Otherwise it must change, too.

Changing your mind is hard.

Changing your habits is harder.

**Changing an organization's culture
is even more difficult.**

Changing your mind and refocusing your attention is a fine first step, but old habits tend to die hard. And even if you can change your habits, your efforts will likely fail in a culture that does not encourage continual improvement of paradigms. To be successful, the culture itself must embrace and encourage this kind of change.

It is therefore my belief that any ongoing success in this area is also dependent upon a transformation of the organization's culture. Traditional leadership philosophies are not suited for this task. It takes a different kind of culture — what will be described as a *Process Control Environment* — to complete the transformation.

Unfortunately, leaders in our larger, more established, and historically most successful organizations have a vested interest in maintaining and sustaining their traditional ways, because they have more to lose and much more to protect. Leading a transformation of this scale is too often viewed as disruptive and not replicable in their culture.

And, to make matters worse, these traditional leadership philosophies are typically housed in well-established *Command and Control Structures* that reinforce and sustain the existing culture. It is as if we humans are held hostage in organizational structures that resist changes in the way we think, and we are, therefore, blinded by our own already deep-seated habits that resulted from our own preconditioned cultural bias.

So, to reiterate, internalizing "foreign" cultural distinctions like these requires the willingness and perseverance to let go of and modify certain pre-existing habits. This in turn requires different just-like references, in order to help re-label, re-frame, re-visualize, and make real a different point of view that will underpin new and improved habits. The caveat is that it can work only in a culture that will accept this new behavior . . . in this case, a *Process Control Environment*. So, traditional leaders must not only let go of their own past habits, and "adopt this new philosophy," they must also dismantle their command and control structures in order that others may follow.

If this sounds circular or recursive, it is. It is certainly not linear.

Nevertheless, it is the way our *reflective* minds process our perceptions of the environment (our point of view) and then automate what *we think* we know, into fast-acting *reflexive* habits — habits that will *fit* the environment. An organizational environment that will accept this type of ongoing change requires a very different leadership philosophy and a very different culture.

This is a difficult idea to internalize, so let me give a couple of quick examples: It's just like the alcoholic who goes to rehab with the best of intentions, and successfully breaks his old habits, but soon discovers that he can no longer hang out with his old drinking buddies. Its just like the young recruit who joins the military, and finds his environmental rug pulled from beneath him the first day of boot camp — he realizes at once that his prior paradigm has changed and new habits are on the way. For the reformed alcoholic, his environment must change for him, or else he must leave the environment. Likewise, in the case of the recruit, when the environment changes, he must change too.

Each of these examples illustrates that these three things — paradigms, habits, and culture — are related. Everything, so it seems, is about relationships.

When strong leadership embraces these relationships and embarks on this mandala-like journey, something magical begins to happen . . . Relationships begin to grow. As we learn to listen carefully to the vision of others, we see that our vision is part of something larger. This does not diminish our sense of responsibility for the vision; it deepens it, and our stewardship for a shared vision allows us to improve our paradigm. The vision ceases to be a possession, as in "this is my vision." It becomes more than an organizational goal — it becomes our aim — "our calling." In this way, shared beliefs create a culture of becoming better, and the transformation begins here.

What Deming called "understanding psychology," I prefer to call "understanding relationships." The next chapter illustrates that focusing more on relationships, and less on stuff, is what really underpins these eastern cultural distinctions and allows for a culture of *continual improvement*. It opens the way for a process control environment.

For right-brained cultures, reality is in the process, and the process is more about relationships than it is about stuff.

Let's face it: the world is filled with contradictions, ambiguities, dichotomies, paradoxes, and disruptive paradigms. If we hold on too tight to just one way of thinking we will, just like those cowboys in *Lonesome Dove*, surely miss something very important. It takes us all . . . both cowboys and Indians. We can no longer afford to be "half-witted" about such important subjects.

CHAPTER FIVE

Understanding Relationships

People don't care how much you know,
until they know how much you care
– John C. Maxwell

Deming's tenet of understanding psychology (or, in my words, understanding relationships) is a prerequisite to transforming traditional (western) leadership philosophies.

A more personal spin on Maxwell's quote sounds something more like a clever quip that Yogi Berra might have made:

If you don't think about people,
how are you going to get them to think about you?

This is not fluff. It is heavy stuff. It is what quantum physicists and neuroscientists are just beginning to sort out and understand. It is a very different paradigm. It's about the relationships that make up our world more so than the stuff that is in our world.

Newton's classical physics is all about stuff. Matter is what matters most. It deals with inanimate objects that can be easily measured with our five senses. It is a left-brained reductionist view of the world in which everything can be reduced to its most basic elements, analyzed and reassembled into a mechanistic model that theoretically can predict the outcome of any transaction. It permeates our western culture.

Quantum physics, on the other hand, is all about relationships. It deals less with causal relations, and much more with co-relations of things we cannot perceive with our five senses — things like force fields instead of stuff, waves instead of particles, and energy instead of matter.

They are both good theories, but to understand one you must in some way let go of the other. Unfortunately, in the case of quantum physics there is very little for us to grab on to.

Quantum physics has been around for over 100 years, but just like the teachings of Deming, it is difficult to comprehend because we have so few "just-like" references (metaphors) to visualize what it is telling us. For most of us, Newton makes perfect sense, and this quantum physics "stuff" sounds like gibberish.

In 1975, Fritjof Capra wrote a groundbreaking book, *The Tao of Physics: An Exploration of the Parallels Between Modern Physics and Eastern Mysticism*. In another book, *The Dancing Wu Li Masters* (1979), Gary Zukav writes about the mystic's interpretations of quantum physics. Both books remain best sellers because they provide valuable just-like references necessary for us to comprehend these — you guessed it — right-brained ideas. [1]

Likewise, modern neuroscience has now determined that even our brains are better explained using this quantum approach.

Let's save the science for the next chapter. First, let's just focus on the main point:

Relationships are more important than stuff.

John Wooden, the famous basketball coach at UCLA, won ten national championships, yet his coaching advice more often emphasized relationships over winning. For instance, he told his players to always thank the teammate who passed the ball after you make a basket. One player asked him how this was possible during the game. Wooden responded, "Just give him a nod or throw him a finger." The player said, "What if he's not looking?" Wooden said, "He will be."

Coach Wooden understood the importance of relationships and his leadership philosophies were a constant reminder. To learn more about Wooden's leadership philosophies, go to Sys-Tao.org/links. You will see that he was always telling us: It is the way we play, and not the score, that matters most.

Transformed leaders must also understand that people would rather solve customer problems than work on company goals. The following cliché speaks to this point:

When I work on problems, I come in early and leave late.
When I work on goals, I come in late and leave early.

Setting company goals puts the focus on what is acceptable (as in minimum standards) and encourages things like: monthly budgets, quotas, incentives, bonuses, performance reviews, employee rankings, and management by objectives. Goals are judgmental. They put the focus on "what should be," and too often they are manipulative. They create unnecessary competition between associates to get "stuff" done, and they invite fear into the workplace.

---

1   Capra's video summary of *The Tao of Physics* can be seen at Sys-Tao.org/links.

Solving customer problems, on the other hand, puts the focus on "what could be." It describes what is most desirable for the customer, something we refer to as *quality consciousness*. It fosters *continual improvement* and it encourages a more subjective approach, described with words like: listen, learn, share; collaboration, cooperation, conversation; dialogue, trust, respect. A focus on solving customer problems is a necessary first step to creating caring relationships in your organization.

These distinctions boil down to understanding the difference between extrinsic and intrinsic motivation. They are paramount to Understanding Relationships. The one influences our behavior in a reflexive or impulsive way, while the other influences us in a more reflective or thoughtful way.

Extrinsic motivation refers to the performance of an activity in order to attain (or avoid) an outcome. Extrinsic motivation comes from outside the individual. It is most often characterized by rewards or punishment . . . the carrot or the stick. It is simple, straightforward and very old-fashioned. Consider a worker who is given a task, with the promise of a specific reward and/or a punishment based on his success in meeting the objective. Certainly, he will be motivated, but most likely it will be for his own sake . . . not for the task itself.

Intrinsic motivation, on the other hand, refers to a sense of fulfillment that comes from an interest or enjoyment in the task itself. It exists within the individual, in a subjective way, and it does not rely on some external pressure — like carrots or sticks — to drive accomplishment. Some say it is too idealistic. I disagree. Consider the same worker given the same task, but this time, he is asked to "go with the flow and focus on solving the customer's problems. If anything goes wrong — just tell us what happened, so that we can improve our process for next time — we need your input."

If you don't think this is a good idea, then you really do need to finish this book. It is my contention that in this situation he will be more creative and more willing to serve his customer, and more likely to help improve the company's process capabilities. He will perform the task for its own sake, and he will grow and become better. He will be intrinsically motivated.

This intrinsic approach to solving customer problems leads to a subjective interpretation of *quality* — namely, quality is defined by whatever the customer deems most desirable . . . whatever the customer values most.

Describing quality in objective terms is difficult, because all customers are unique. But if your "process capability" can operate inside the most stringent of their specification limits, you can be sure that you're able to meet or exceed all of your customers' desires. There is a fabled story of a Japanese manufacturer who received an order for 10,000 bolts from an American customer. The customer specified that no more than 0.1% "out of spec" would be acceptable. By way of a misunderstanding, the Japanese supplier sent two containers — a large one with 10,000 perfect bolts, and a smaller one with 10 "out of spec" bolts. Clearly the Japanese supplier had adequate process capability, but because he operated under the concept of "desirability," he misinterpreted the American's concept of "acceptability." The supplier had no concept of a minimum standard, and so he assumed that his American customer, for some reason, also wanted these 10 too-large or too-small bolts. And he delivered.

The Japanese bolt maker in this story understands something that is lost on many westerners:

Reality is in the process, not the results.

The traditional western approach to quality would be along the lines of some form of inspection to assure that no more than 0.1% of the bolts were out of spec. Measuring process capability, on the other hand, suggests that we can predict in objective terms whether our process can deliver quality. But measuring the process, and not the results, is counterintuitive and antithetical to the traditional western mindset.

Besides, measuring a process is not easy. How do you do it? It is common sense that our measures must predict the capability of the process if we are to deliver quality, but how do you measure a process? These are questions that will be answered later when we are ready to discuss the important subject of understanding variation — which, by the way, has a lot to do with relationships.

Nevertheless, it is common practice for traditional leaders to do what is easy; they measure the results and hold the people accountable with extrinsic motivators. It does nothing to improve the process, but it does affect the people. It creates fear, reduces teamwork, creates barriers, and removes joy from the work force.

You can improve the process, but you can't improve results.

Competition *with* associates to create processes capable of solving intrinsic (subjective) customer problems is very different from competition *between* associates to reach an extrinsic (objective) company goal.

Working on "what could be" creates constructive conflict and long-term joy. Working on "what should be" creates instant gratification but long-term pain. The one promotes self-esteem and teamwork, and the other destroys them and creates stress in their place.

Six of Deming's 14 points (points 7 through 12) refer specifically to this concept. Consider for example points 8 & 9:

8. **Drive out fear, so that everyone may work effectively for the company.**

9. **Break down barriers between departments. People in research, design, sales, and production must work as a team, to foresee problems, in production and in use that may be encountered with the product or service.**

The past, "what was," is filled with time-tested paradigms that may or may not be predictive of future events. Memories of past success will always be a source of pride. The past is a fertile ground for "what should be" thinking, and it is a ready source for arrogance. It sets the standard based on what is acceptable, it is influenced mostly by extrinsic motivation, and it relies heavily on past habits. Deming referred to this type behavior as "recycling ignorance." I call it "paving over cow paths."

The future, "what could be," is unknown, and therefore, constantly in need of improved paradigms that can better predict what is just ahead. This is the essence of solving customer problems and being quality conscious. The focus here is on what is most desirable, and the motivation is far more intrinsic.

It requires us to slow down, to be more empathic, and to challenge our old habits, which are housed in the most primitive, least flexible and fastest-reacting parts of our brain.

We live in the present, "what is," and whether we choose "what was" or "what could be" as our frame of reference, there is a gap filled with words like the ones shown here. I call it the "emotional gap" for reasons that will be discussed in the next chapter.

PAST	PRESENT	FUTURE
What	What	What
"Was"	**"Is"**	**"Could Be"**

The Emotional Gaps

PICK ONE

Pride & Arrogance	Continual Improvement
Instant Gratification	Constructive Conflict
Long Term Pain	Long Term Joy
Acceptability	Desirability

In later life, Deming substituted the word "joy" for the word "pride." He realized that *pride* is one of the Seven Deadly Sins, and it has nothing to do with "Understanding Psychology." Pride is a result of past accomplishments. You can't improve results — they are in the past. Joy is simply the journey of becoming better. You can always improve the process.

Each of us remembers the past differently, from our own personal point of view, but together, we can share a common vision of the future. Thought about in this way, it is the past that is unpredictable.

Neither Deming nor Coach Wooden could possibly have understood the neuroscience that explains their philosophies, because it had not yet been discovered. The next chapter delves lightly into how this rapidly evolving science seems to support what they knew instinctively — how we learn and how we are motivated.

CHAPTER SIX

The Neuroscience of Learning
and Motivation

I must study politics and war, that our sons may have liberty to study mathematics and philosophy. Our sons ought to study mathematics and philosophy, geography, natural history and naval architecture, navigation, commerce and agriculture in order to give their children a right to study painting, poetry, music, architecture, statuary, tapestry and porcelain.

JOHN ADAMS
Letter to Abigail Adams
May 12, 1780

Adams' progression of thoughts is similar to the following chart representing Abraham Maslow's 1943 Theory of Motivation. Maslow's theory is commonly referred to as "The Hierarchy of Needs."

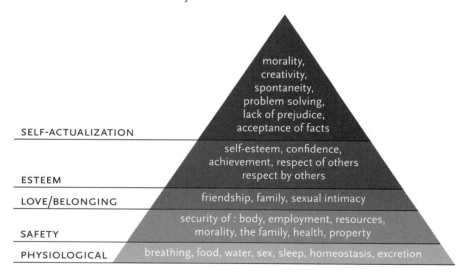

SELF-ACTUALIZATION — morality, creativity, spontaneity, problem solving, lack of prejudice, acceptance of facts

ESTEEM — self-esteem, confidence, achievement, respect of others respect by others

LOVE/BELONGING — friendship, family, sexual intimacy

SAFETY — security of : body, employment, resources, morality, the family, health, property

PHYSIOLOGICAL — breathing, food, water, sex, sleep, homeostasis, excretion

Both of these men seemed to be suggesting, in their own manner of speaking, that "extrinsic needs" must come first, before we can pursue "intrinsic needs." Neither of them makes an explicit or even a qualitative distinction regarding how we are motivated, much less how we learn. Both men simply suggest that there is a linear pecking order or hierarchical structure for what these things are that we pursue.

It reminds me of an anecdote: Supposedly, a well-known scientist (some say it was Bertrand Russell) once gave a public lecture on astronomy. He described how the earth orbits around the sun and how the sun, in turn, orbits around the center of a vast collection of stars called our galaxy. At the end of the lecture, a little old lady at the back of the room got up and said: "What you have told us is rubbish. The world is really a flat plate supported on the back of a giant tortoise." The scientist gave a superior smile before replying, "What is the tortoise standing on?" "You're very clever, young man, very clever," said the old lady. "But it's turtles all the way down!"

For several hundred years now, it has been pretty much accepted that we learn by instruction and that we are motivated by rewards and punishment "all the way up."

Neuroscientists have recently discovered that this is just not so. Instead, we learn by "selection" more so than by "instruction," and there really is such a thing as "intrinsic motivation."

Let me explain by starting with a question: How do you intrinsically motivate someone? The answer is that you stop extrinsically motivating them. In order to appreciate this rather flippant answer, we need to understand what is meant by the statement "We learn by *selection* more so than by *instruction*."

Our traditional Newtonian view of how we learn was to envision our five senses as recording devices that, like a camera or a microphone, take in what's out there in our world and somehow store it in our brain. Education, traditionally, has pretty much forced stuff at us and it has been our job to memorize it. Our motivation, of course was the carrots and sticks associated with school.

Neuroscientists, just like quantum physicists, have determined that it is the relationships more than the stuff or the carrots or the sticks that explains how we learn. Let me digress in order to explain.

In his 1859 book, *On the Origin of the Species*, Charles Darwin theorized that evolution is based on what he called "natural selection." His theory predates modern genetics by nearly 100 years, but Darwin put his finger on what today we know to be true. It is our relationship with the environment that has allowed our genetic make-up to learn to survive and evolve.

There is huge diversity in our genetic make-up, so it is understandable that small random changes evolve with our common descent from generation to generation. We all know that mankind has for centuries been able to modify the genetic make-up of countless domesticated plants and animals through the process of selective breeding. Darwin took this "just-like" reference and reasoned that nature did the same thing by increasing the probability of survival for those species that best *fit in* with their environment. He was not speaking of physical fitness when he suggested "survival of the fittest;" he was suggesting survival of those that *fit best* with the environment.

After millions of years of this type of genetic learning and evolution, it turns out that we humans have actually developed three brains, ranging in archaeological age from 350 million years ago to just 50 thousand years ago.

I have already discussed some of the distinctions in how the two hemispheres of our brain process information differently, but most scholars would also agree that this process of natural selection has evolved our brains into what they refer to as the *triune brain*. Almost literally, as we evolved, we added two new brains on top of our original equipment.

It is generally accepted that higher levels of proactive thinking (language, abstract thought, imagination, and consciousness) occur on the top — our human brain (or *neo-cortex*) — while the faster-reacting, more rigid and most compulsive activity occurs on the bottom — our reptilian brain (or *basal ganglia*) and in the middle — our mammalian brain (or *limbic system*) — which deals more with our feelings of emotion and our value judgments. This is an oversimplification, of course, but it is accurate, and my promise was to only delve lightly into this heady subject.

Consider this conceptual rendering of our triune brain in which I have taken the liberty to rename our three brains:

It is generally agreed that most of the incoming sensory information, from our five senses, is first processed by our *Feeler* and sent instantly on to our *Thinker* and our *Doer*.

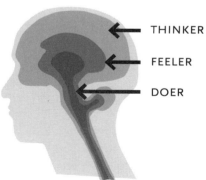

THINKER

FEELER

DOER

Our thinker operates relatively slowly, and it compares the new information to other "just-like" references (memories) and reflects on the relationships in order to draw new conclusions. It is a very *selective* operation in which patterns of data that do not *fit* are leveled out, and that which does *fit* is sharpened up and assimilated into a story that makes more sense than what was previously understood to be the "truth." It is a kind of fractal-like growth of neurons that continually branch out and add more and more complex patterns of networking information about subjects that are more and more meaningful to that individual — it is intrinsic learning. It cannot exist in thin air, but must attach itself to existing physical structures, which represent previously learned information. What this means is that all new learning is dependent upon internal self-referral — that is, on what we already think we know and hold meaningful. Needless to say, this emerging complexity lends itself to non-threatening circumstances that do not require an instant response.

Our doer, on the other hand, operates extremely quickly and it is almost entirely reflexive — its network has far fewer neurons. It relies on deep-seated habits (based on previously learned environmental relationships) as well as inherited (genetically learned) instincts. It is a stress-driven system tied closely to immanent predatory danger. Jokingly, it is often explained by its association with the four "F's" — fight, flight, food, and . . . reproduction. Our feeler and our doer, therefore, work powerfully together in an almost instantaneous way in order to keep us from harm's way or to enable us to seize an opportunity when it is presented to us.

Because this feeler/doer combination is faster and enhances survival, it is also the default, or go-to, system. Then, if the situation does not require an immediate (extrinsic) response, attention can be upshifted to our thinker for a more reflective (intrinsic) response.

Our primitive, fast-acting feeler/doer response system works well when sudden forceful reactive action is necessary. There is nothing wrong with a little stress in these situations. Likewise, in most stress-free situations, it is a very good thing that we can rely on our habits to get us through the day without having to think about how to get up, get dressed, go to work, prepare a meal, etc.

Too often, though, our feeler/doer spring into action unnecessarily and respond fearfully, impulsively, or inappropriately to situations that don't require an immediate response. Carrots and sticks institutionalize this type of behavior and inhibit our ability to upshift attention to our thinker. The resulting chemical responses in our brain — most often associated with dopamine — actually strengthen our feeler's reaction to the situation and dampen our thinker's ability to get involved with the situation. Our sub-conscious doer just plows ahead mindlessly. We become fearful of or even addicted to the situation, but we don't know why. We learn nothing from these experiences, because we have no theory — we have not involved our thinker.

On the other hand, if our environment is relatively free of fear and free of unnecessary extrinsic motivators, our slower-acting thinker can more easily and more often get involved. It can soften or even override our reflexive doer's response and come up with a better solution — if given time to respond, it can make sense of our senses.

In summary, *extrinsic motivation* increases fear, anxiety, and stress; and it impedes the thoughtful use of the more advanced parts of our brain. It is difficult to develop new and improved paradigms when excessive extrinsic motivation traps us in our old paradigm and our preexisting habitual patterns of behavior. Benjamin Franklin said it this way: "Tell me and I forget. Teach me and I remember. Involve me and I learn."

It is easy to understand why both Deming and Coach Wooden admonished dependence on extrinsic motivators. Their existence "tampers" with (adds unnecessary noise to) the natural stimulation coming from what Deming called "the voice of the process" — Coach Wooden would just call it "the game."

The importance of harmony among our three brains is captured in Gary Zukav's 1989 best-selling book, *The Seat of the Soul*:

> When we align our thoughts, emotions, and actions with the
> highest part of ourselves, we are filled with enthusiasm, purpose, &
> meaning. Life is rich & full. We have no thoughts of bitterness. We
> have no memory of fear. We are joyous & intimately engaged with
> our world. This is the experience of authentic power.

But there is more. Remember the grandmaster chess player discussed earlier? What was really going on in his brain as he perfected his game and developed "just-like" references for other aspects of his life is an example of what neuroscientists now call neuroplasticity. It is what I have called selective learning — his thinker levels, sharpens, and assimilates new information into a story that is intrinsically meaningful to him. As his neurons react with the environment, they literally "fire together and wire together." We literally and physically change our minds when we react with our environment — when we learn.

There is, of course, a paradoxical caveat: When we try to learn in the traditional ways using instruction, and carrots and sticks, we all too often miss what is intrinsically meaningful to our thinker, causing worry. Instead we divert unnecessary attention to our doer, causing stress, and we create anxiety in our feeler as our brain goes unnecessarily out of sync. We have created what I call an "emotional gap." It is the opposite of what Gary Zukav referred to in the above quote. It is, in fact, a cue that our habits are not in sync with our values and our core beliefs. As explained above, there are times when it is best to rely on our fast-acting feeler/doer, but when we are in the process of learning, improving the processes of life, and being creative, it is best to set the extrinsic motivators aside and allow our thinkers to do what comes naturally and pursue the task for its own sake.

Based on this, one might challenge the profit motive as being too extrinsic and argue that we should all be more intrinsically directed to some higher purpose motive. Surely that is not where this book is headed. Is this is a business book or is it some spiritual journey? Well, in a sense it is both.

So, what is the mission really?

FURTHER LEARNING

Daniel Pink's videos based on his books: *A Whole New Mind*, 2005; and *Drive: The Surprising Truth About What Motivates Us*, 2009, shed further light on the subject of this chapter. Daniel Kahneman's 2011 book, *Thinking, Fast and Slow*, adds even more credence to these concepts. His interview with Charlie Rose is a good synopsis of this important book. (Sys-Tao.org/links)

CHAPTER SEVEN

Mission Statements

Common Sense that is not Common Practice is a
Paradox.

— Eliyahu Goldratt

Paradox defined: *Paradox is used in a particular way within the
literature of economics to describe situations in which apparent
facts are in conflict with models or theories (paradigms) to
which some class of people hold allegiance. This use of the word,
paradox, implies a strong belief in both the measured facts, and
in the paradigm. The resolution to economic paradoxes tends to
be of the form that the data does not fit the paradigm, or the
data is not correct or, (the most common case) the paradigm
does not fit the environment measured.*

— Wikipedia

Goldratt's quote and this definition of a paradox, when taken together as
a single concept, describe analogically what I have referred to as our "thinker,
feeler, and doer." *Common sense* and *common practice* are clearly analogous
to "our thinker" and "our doer" (our habits); and when they go out of sync
with our perception of our environment we are faced with an emotional gap,
a paradox, that causes "our feeler" (our emotions) to kick in (e.g. we tend to
laugh or become angry.) It is our biological signal that something is not right.

Mission statements are often a very good example of this sort of a dilemma.
They tend to be rather lofty expressions handed down from higher authority,
and like the adults in the fairy tale, "The Emperor's New Clothes," which
is about "the king that had no clothes," we more often than not accept the
paradox, restrain our emotions, avoid common sense, and pay allegiance to the
naked emperor as our common practice.

The paradox in most mission statements is that they typically steer us in seemingly conflicting directions regarding *what* to do, but provide little advice regarding *how* to resolve the dilemma.

For instance, business literature is full of phrases suggesting that the customer is king and customer service is everything. This *purpose motive* is especially popular if your point of view is from Main Street. Nevertheless, a more popular point of view from Wall Street is that maximizing profits and increasing shareholder wealth is the primary goal of businesses. From this more materialistic point of view, customers are more like a source of funds than "kings."

What should we focus on — customer satisfaction or making money? Could it be that this purpose motive is even more important than the profit motive? Maybe Coach Wooden was right; it is the way we play, and not the score, that matters most. Could it be that what we aim for is more important than what we achieve? What is the *mission*, really? How can this paradox be resolved? [1] Some people say, "do both," but the paradox is not resolved. *How* can we do both without compromising either?

Clearly, American industry was having difficulty with this dilemma in 1980, as evidenced by that question, "If Japan can, why can't we?" And we at Great Plains were unaware of the so-called "quality revolution" for nearly ten years after that. It was not until about 1990 that we began to understand the way out of this riddle.

It was at that time that we began to focus on the *how*. It became my belief that if we focused on the how, the process would naturally improve, and we would always be prepared to accomplish *what* ever came before us.

Our mission statement was simplified. It read in part ". . . to quench the thirst of our customer's customer." Clearly, our focus sided with the customer. This of course doesn't answer any questions, but it does provide a point of view and a starting point.

---

1 In his 2012 book, *How will you measure your life?*, Harvard Professor Clayton M. Christensen explains why he would agree that purpose is more important than profit. And, in his most famous book, *The Innovator's Dilemma*, (1999), he explains why "success" so often sows the seeds for failure. (Sys-Tao.org/links)

But when I said, "our employees are customers too," they greeted this good news with yawns and under-the-breath sarcastic expressions. They seemed to know instinctively that just because I had changed my mind, it was no indication that the rest of the bosses would change their habits.

I also said "we are each other's customers," and that we should refer to each other as "associates or colleagues, and not employees or employers." I liked to say no one is "just" a worker and no one is "over" anyone; we are all associates, working together to solve our customers' problems.

Intellectually, this suggests a chain of customers: consumers, shoppers, retail customers, internal customers, and suppliers. Practically speaking, however, our bosses were still trapped in their habitual past and unwilling to let go of their control over those traditional organizational silos.

These examples might seem like failed attempts at "Servant Leadership" or idealistic platitudes — too good to be true, too far out to be real — so let me be clear, these are beliefs and aspirations. But, mission statements are about what "could be" and not necessarily about "what is." After all, we must do more than just change our minds; we must change our habits too, and that takes time. It is an ongoing and never-ending process. That's why the next part of our mission statement was so important. It is about continual improvement.

So, the next part of our mission statement was modified to read, "We live to become better . . ." This did not imply "better than someone else;" it simply suggested improvement.

It is my belief that most associates, even bosses, really don't care very much about shareholder wealth, but that everyone would like to become better at what they do. Some social scientists call this "mastery;" I call it common sense.

It follows that since every one of our associates chose Great Plains as a place to work, a worthwhile aim for all of us would be to always get better at taking care of our own internal customers until we finally "quench the thirst" of all of our customers' customers. Some social scientists call this "purpose;" I call it common sense.

Said in this way, we had a mission statement that everyone could agree on, and we had a job description that applied to everyone. The only thing a new associate had to do was get to know his customer and take care of her needs. Some social scientists call this "autonomy;" I call it common sense.

The focus gradually shifted from selling stuff and making money to building relationships and solving problems. Of course, we assumed that we would continue to sell a few Cokes and make a little money, but we had changed our aim.

Becoming better at internal customer service requires precise processes all along the chain of customers, but when associates focus on just "their" process as in a traditional organizational structure, it tends to create islands of excellence housed in silos that actually destroy these caring relationships. Quality consciousness — the voice of the customer — gets lost in the shuffle, and the system as a whole loses precision.

On the other hand, when relationships become more caring, the total process naturally becomes more precise and more capable of fulfilling our customers' desires.

The nurturing of these caring customer relationships among associates is difficult, and it became our management's most important job. Said another way, as we loosened formal company controls, we had to tighten our interpersonal relationships.

The traditional command and control organizational structure would have to change too. Changing your mind is one thing, changing your habits is also important, but changing the organization's culture would be the hardest thing of all.

How we accomplished this important job will be explained later, but first, let's address this old cliché:

What gets measured gets done.

There are lots of metrics to measure company profits and shareholder wealth, but what metrics are there to measure our *capability* to provide customer satisfaction? How did we know if our "thirst-quenching" capability was working? And, how did we reconcile a mission statement that requires satisfaction and happiness for customers as well as financial success for the company and its shareholders? How did we square these seemingly disparate ideas?

As a friend once told me, "I will explain it to you, but I can't understand it for you." To understand it, you must change your perception of the truth, your paradigm, your mental model, or as Deming would say; it has to do with the Theory of Knowledge. If you want to understand the way out of this paradox, you must literally change your mind.

Then, in order to change your ways and transform this new understanding into common practice, you will also have to deal with your limbic system and that reptilian part of your brain that controls your habits.

Old habits die hard, and it takes "constancy of purpose" to create new habits that will reinforce new paradigms. New habits require different metaphors and new "just-like" references. You must resist the tendency to make "right or true" that which is merely familiar, and make "wrong or false" that which is only strange.

Finally, to make this new understanding operational, your environment, the culture of your organization, must embrace and encourage the continual improvement of paradigms.

Changing your mind is hard.
Changing your habits is harder.
Changing an organization's culture
is even more difficult.

The resolution to this mission statement paradox begins with *thruput accounting,* a concept first developed by Eliyahu Goldratt in his 1984 book, *The Goal.*

I realize that *thruput* is misspelled here, but that is just the abbreviated way we always spelled it at Great Plains.

Spelled this way, it became a metaphor for something very different than our traditional management accounting paradigms. Understanding this strange new word allows us to better appreciate the short-comings of the more familiar word, "cost," and it is

ELIYAHU GOLDRATT

our traditional "cost paradigm" that must change if we want to resolve the paradox of a mission statement that focuses on both:

Customer satisfaction and happiness,
and . . .
Financial success for the company and its shareholders.

FURTHER READING

Relevance Lost: The Rise and fall of Management Accounting, by Thomas Johnson and Robert Kaplan, details the history of management accounting in America and how it has lost its relevance. Their 1987 classic accurately explains the problem, but it gives few answers. Goldratt's 1984 book may well be the solution.

Ironically, Johnson and Kaplan parted ways after writing their landmark book. In 1992, Johnson wrote *Relevance Regained: From Top-Down Control to Bottom-Up Empowerment,* which very much parallels the tenets of *Sys-Tao.* On the other hand, in 1997, Kaplan wrote: *Cost & Effect: Using Integrated Cost Systems to Drive Profitability and Performance.* It pioneered the concept of "Activity Based Accounting," an approach neither Goldratt, Deming, nor I would ever endorse (*see* **Appendix II**). Kaplan, so it seems, has followed the traditional route while Johnson has pursued the road less traveled, which I believe to be a better way. An interesting article on their philosophical differences can be found at Sys-Tao. org/links.

CHAPTER EIGHT

Cost is a Four Letter Word

Thruput is good for everyone.

Thruput is an important step towards reconciling the paradox between disparate mission statements that seem to favor either shareholders or customers. Maximizing *thruput* over time is good for everyone . . . both shareholders and customers.

"Thruput" is simply the selling price minus the ingredients of a perfect Coke. A bottle of Coke is made up only of the bottle, the secret formula, and the cap. That's what we call "product cost." Said another way, thruput is the premium a customer pays in addition to this common sense definition of the cost of a Coke, "product cost."

Envision a lemonade stand that you may have had when you were a kid. Thruput is what was left of the nickel you probably received after paying for the cup and the lemonade you put into it. Thruput in this case was probably about four cents.

Generally Accepted Accounting Principles (GAAP) allocate all sorts of other costs to Cokes — things like labor overhead and depreciation — and they would do it to the lemonade too, if the kids would let them. In many ways the kids are smarter, so let's stick with the thruput idea for now.

Thruput (net sales minus product costs) is the money coming into the company every time we sell a Coke. And, because thruput is the premium paid in addition to the product cost of a perfect product, it is *over time* an objective measure of *customer value* — how much customers value Cokes, or lemonade, or anything.

Thruput per hour — product flow — is what really matters. Thruput per unit tells us very little. The rate at which consumers enjoy Coca-Cola is a good measure of their satisfaction over time, and it is of course also a measure of the money coming into the company.

The notion of a perfect Coke is important, because customers don't value those other things, that GAAP accountants hide inside what they call "cost of goods sold" (COGS). Net sales minus COGS is what they call "gross profit." Thruput is a larger number and a simpler concept than gross profit. The gross profit of your lemonade stand was probably only about two cents. It's a good thing you didn't know that, or you probably wouldn't have opened the lemonade stand in the first place.

More importantly, thruput measures customer satisfaction; gross profit does not. Customers just don't care about the things accountants allocate to their lemonade, because they don't drink allocated costs.

There is no paradox concerning the rate at which we generate thruput. And, it is easier to focus on quality consciousness and the intrinsic nature of solving customer problems when all associates understand thruput in this win/win sort of way.

Then, all _cash_ expenses that are not part of the ingredients of the perfect Cokes we sold can be added up and called *total operating expense* (TOE). It's what you might have paid the kid next door to help you run the lemonade stand, and of course that lemonade you so often spilled along the way.

GAAP accounting hides some of these expenses inside gross profit. Total operating expense, on the other hand, is the cash operating cost of the total system. It is the cost of "The Process." It measures all of "the money going out" of the company over time, while thruput measures both customer value and all of "the money coming in" to the company over time.

Thruput is good for everyone, both shareholders and customers, so in this way the mission statement paradox is relegated to the TOE. The paradox seems to be 100% inside the process — the money going out (cash operating expenses). This is an important first step: The problem has been isolated, it is clearly visible, and we know the size of it.

Thruput minus total operating expenses (TOE) equals what we call *cash operating profit* (COP). It is exactly the same number that financial people call EBITDA *(earnings before interest, taxes, depreciation, and amortization)*. Cash Operating Profit is just simpler, more descriptive, and easier to understand. Both terms (EBITDA and COP) tell us how much money is left over after operations.

Net Sales

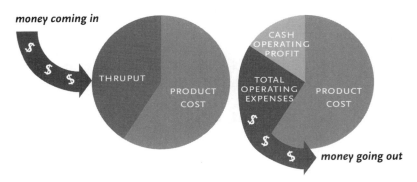

Appendix II dives a bit deeper into the ramifications of the differences in Generally Accepted Accounting Principles and Thruput Accounting. This graphic, on the other hand, illustrates the straightforward simplicity of Thruput Accounting.

For now, suffice it to say that when we only use GAAP Accounting, it is difficult to know total operating expenses (TOE). Let me say it again: It is difficult to know the cost of the process using GAAP Accounting.

Nevertheless, Thruput Accounting can only tell us the size of the total operating expense. There are still more questions:

- **Why would a customer be happy to pay more for one product than for another if the product costs are the same?**

- **Even if you sold a product for less, would the increased volume generate enough thruput over time to cover your TOE?**

- **What does it "cost" to bring the product to market?**

The short answer to these questions is that the "cost" of the process, what we have called total cash operating expenses (TOE), is like cholesterol; there are "good" costs and there are "bad" costs.

The good costs add customer value, and they are the reason customers are so often willing to pay a premium in addition to the "product costs" over time. We call these good costs "capability."

Everything in the TOE that is not capability represents the bad costs. We call these bad costs "waste," and they, of course, should be eliminated.

Thought about in this way, the paradox is defined, but not resolved, because no accounting system can separate the good costs from the bad costs. All accounting can do is catalogue, sum up, and allocate these costs.

But allocating costs just recreates the paradox we are trying to resolve. And cataloging costs into functional areas, described by a traditional organizational structure, encourages associates to focus on just "their" costs. It becomes increasingly difficult to differentiate these *waste/capability* relationships because they rapidly become the possessions of competing cost-centered bosses.

Thruput Accounting can tell us the size of the total operating expense, but no accounting system can separate *capability* from *waste*.

It might seem like the smaller the total operating expense, the larger the cash operating profit (EBITDA), but what if we whack capability? Then, we might lose thruput over time. Or, what if we increased the total operating expense by adding capability? Then thruput might increase even more. And, if we reduced waste and increased capability the same amount, then over time both thruput and COP would surely go up.

Accounting can't help us when it comes to waste and capability, and to make matters worse, there is a third kind of money. In addition to "the money coming in" (thruput) and "the money going out" (TOE), there is "the money stuck inside." In the case of your lemonade stand it is your pitcher of lemonade, the table Mom loaned you, and your sign. It is what accountants call, "capital costs," and, guess what — it is made up of "good costs" and "bad costs" too!

Separating the good costs and bad costs requires an understanding of "how" the system works as a process, rather than "to whom" or "to what" the costs are allocated. These are the reasons why "cost" is just another four letter word that I try not to use whenever possible.

Thruput is an easy concept to understand, to embrace, and to implement, but *cost* is a difficult paradigm to set aside and use less (pun intended).

Admittedly, accounting can't distinguish the difference between good costs and bad costs. And, because of our deep-seated habits, it is hard to resist managing based on *The Cost Paradigm*.

There is no wonder that it is a common practice for traditional leaders to allocate costs, measure results, and then hold their people accountable using extrinsic methods of motivation — a.k.a. "carrots and sticks." It is easier to do, and, for the most part, traditional leaders have no idea how to measure the capability of the process.

So, how can we measure the process? How can we separate the "good" costs from the "bad" costs? How can we resolve the paradox of a mission statement that focuses on customer satisfaction and happiness, as well as the need for financial success for the company and its shareholders?

We need a different paradigm. We will call it *The Time Paradigm*. It should be noted, however, that the time paradigm does not work well in a *command and control structure* associated with traditional leadership philosophies and GAAP accounting. Instead, it works naturally in a *process control environment* using thruput accounting.

In fact, a process control environment depends on principles like those found in the time paradigm, and these same principles, in turn, complement what Deming called *Understanding Variation*. But first, I should explain what is meant by the term "process control environment."

CHAPTER NINE

A Process Control Environment

Changing traditional leadership philosophies begins with a holistic systems view of the organization. The emphasis shifts from a closed *Command and Control Structure* to an open *Process Control Environment*. The organization becomes more like a living organism made up of a chain of customers.

In a metaphorical way, the "DNA" of all processes is the same. They all have the same molecular structure as indicated in our medallion above and as shown in the diagram below.

The medallion was incorporated in all of our service awards, which were given to our associates for every five years of continuous customer service. It symbolizes the concepts of this chapter.

Information is constantly flowing from left to right across the top, and stuff (goods and services) is constantly flowing from the right to the left across the bottom. It does not matter what you name the boxes. Sourcing comes from the right and fulfillment happens on the left.

This diagram was first drawn with green arrows and blue boxes. The nomenclature clicked. The words *green arrows* and *blue boxes* soon took on special meaning. It is now understood: every green arrow is a relationship, and every blue box is a customer.

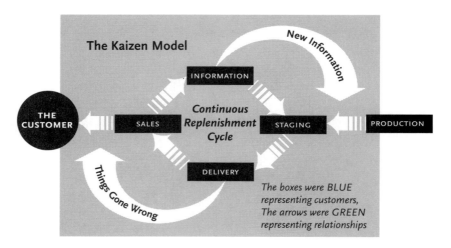

The Kaizen Model

Continuous Replenishment Cycle

INFORMATION

THE CUSTOMER

SALES

STAGING

PRODUCTION

DELIVERY

New Information

Things Gone Wrong

The boxes were BLUE representing customers,
The arrows were GREEN representing relationships

Three things are always happening inside this molecular model:

> First, and most obvious, is the *replenishment cycle*; replacing the goods and services from the previous cycle.

> Second is the constant influx of *new information* that tells the process to do something different. New information typically creates *special cause variations* that disrupt the precision of the replenishment cycle.

> Third is the coping mechanism that deals with the inevitability of TGWs, *things gone wrong*. In a similar way, TGWs typically create *common cause variations* that also disrupt the natural rhythm, the precision, of the replenishment cycle.

The *variations* will be discussed later, but for now just think of these three things as being analogous to a sewing-machine-like system that is alive and continuously replenishing stitches, but is always confronted with the possibility of the thread breaking or the machine jamming (things gone wrong). Likewise, there is always the possibility that someone will want to change the color of the thread or adjust the stitch in some new way (new information).

A good process can replenish precisely with a high degree of predictability. A great process can also respond quickly and predictably to new information, while coping with the inevitable TGWs, all in a single seamless process as if there were real-time collaboration going on all the time between the blue boxes. A truly great process is never just doing things; it is always learning, evolving, and becoming better.

If you were to zoom in to any of these blue boxes, you'd see more of these kaizen molecules. Just like drilling down inside a fractal — you always see the same repeating pattern. Likewise, these molecules can be linked up to make a *supply chain* or a *demand chain*, depending on your point of view. The demand chain point of view fits better with our mission . . . to quench the thirst of our customer's customers.

It should be obvious that any goods or any services could flow down this chain. Cokes just happen to be easy to understand, and they provide a valuable historical perspective, because they have been around for such a very long time. Furthermore, I happen to be an industry expert when it comes to Cokes, but the principles in this book are transferable to any industry and any organization.

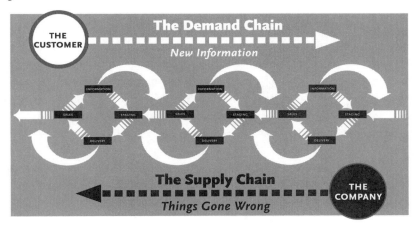

In our case, if you follow these process steps, just like a chain of customers, you can make your way from some well satisfied happy consumer's refrigerator, somewhere in Oklahoma, all the way back along the demand chain to Atlanta, Georgia's world headquarters of The Coca-Cola Company.

We named this biological metaphor of a customer service molecule "The Kaizen Model," because *kaizen* is a Japanese word meaning "continual change for the better." Specifically, it refers to what we would call *continual improvement* or "becoming better." It reminds me of that old advertising jingle, "Things go better with Coke."

Another way to understand this model is to figuratively staple yourself to an order and go with the flow as the order makes its way up the demand chain. Every blue box is full of internal customers hoping for satisfaction and happiness from their supplier associates on the other end of the green arrows.

The blue boxes represent the more structured working parts of the system, and it is understood that the workings of these parts must be precise in order to deliver specified results. It is a left-brained western concept that isn't hard to understand for most of us.

The green arrows, on the other hand, represent organic relationships in need of constant feedback, and it is understood that these relationships must be *caring*. This is a little more right-brained, and it really tugs at our traditional western mindset when we say that these people don't work for their boss; instead, they work to satisfy some co-worker at the tip end of a green arrow in some other boss's blue box. This notion smacks of what has been called *quality consciousness*. The focus is more subjective, the motivation is more intrinsic, and the concept is more holistic. It is about improving the process, in contrast to increasing objective outcomes in each blue box.

In a traditional command and control structure, the bosses manage their people and get results by increasing the productivity of their own blue box.

As a result, silos develop and become "barriers that rob the hourly worker of his right to pride (joy) of workmanship." Additionally, there is typically a great deal of emphasis on *management by objectives* and merit pay (incentives), two things Deming said should be abolished. "Inspect what you expect" too often becomes a management mantra, but again Deming tells us "to cease dependence on inspections."

Just why Deming was so opposed to these traditional leadership philosophies is illustrated by two of his best-known lectures, "The Parable of the Red Beads," and "The Funnel Experiment." Both of these are discussed in **Appendix III**, and a brief clip of Dr. Deming actually performing the Red Bead Experiment can be seen at Sys-Tao.org/links.

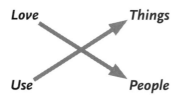

Figuratively speaking, western bosses love their blue boxes and manage their people. The *supply chain* is a fitting term under these conditions, because the focus is on accomplishing supplier goals rather than solving customer problems.

The kaizen model suggests that holistic precision requires caring relationships, and that these caring relationships are what allow the *total* process to become precise. The boss's job shifts from managing people by objectives to managing the process for improvement. Similarly, for the workers, doing what is *acceptable* for their boss gives way to doing what is *desirable* for their customer.

Symbolically, if the relationships are collaborative, the green arrows become short and the entire model hums along "in perfect harmony" — just like another Coke jingle.

It really is better to give than to receive — in this case, giving intrinsic service to customers is better than receiving extrinsic incentives from bosses.

Associates quickly learn that respect is a gift and not something to be earned. When we give respect to each other and respect the process, we gain trust. It is not the other way 'round. When we demand respect we lose trust, and the process control environment reverts quickly back to a command and control structure.

The mission is to become better and make it easier to satisfy the needs of our customer's customer. It takes everyone to improve the process. Quality consciousness is being aware of what the customer wants, and acting on it. Everyone must be free from fear in order to be willing to "take" responsibility and act on it — just like granddad did over 100 years ago when he realized that "responsibility is the only thing you can steal and get away with it." A process control environment enables this. A command and control structure inhibits it.

Let's face it: we westerners are by nature *cowboys*, but when we focus on customer issues and care about people; it engages our whole brain. It brings out both the cowboy and the Indian in each of us and creates a more holistic view of the issues, as well as a more tolerant understanding of the people.

Understanding the green arrows has to do with *understanding relationships*. It re-engages the right side of our brain. It de-emphasizes our habitual dependence on the more primitive parts of our brain. It allows for a more thoughtful, empathic, and inclusive point of view.

The following graphic illustrates the interdependencies between *Precise Systems* and *Caring Relationships*.

Continual Improvement

Caring Relationships	Precise Systems
allow	*require*
Precise Systems	Caring Relationships

- LESS INVENTORY
- LESS APPROVALS
- LESS INSPECTIONS
- LESS WASTE
- LESS CYCLE TIME
- MORE ON TIME
- MORE QUALITY

- SHARED VISION
- TRUST & RESPECT
- COOPERATION
- INTERDEPENDENCE
- FREE OF FEAR & BLAME
- SHARED RESPONSIBILITY
- WIN/WIN TEAMWORK

COWBOYS
BLUE BOXES

INDIANS
GREEN ARROWS

CUSTOMERS   SUPPLIERS

Despite all of this, we sometimes regress, and too much of the cowboy comes out in our actions. Old habits don't die; they just hibernate.

In stressful times we all tend to revert to our past experience, and instinctively call on the most primitive parts of our brain. It is as if we are again just *recycling ignorance.*

In the *Tao Te Ching*, Lao Tzu warns against this type of behavior. He seems to be telling us what can happen when our *thinker,* our *feeler,* and our *doer* go out of sync and destroy these caring relationships. His advice is simple — It is best when "delicate facilitations far outnumber harsh interventions."

HARSH INTERVENTIONS

There are times when it seems as if one must intervene powerfully, suddenly, and even harshly. The wise leader does this only when all else fails.

As a rule, the leader feels more wholesome when the group process is flowing freely and unfolding naturally, when delicate facilitations far outnumber harsh interventions.

Harsh interventions are a warning that the leader may be un-centered or have an emotional attachment to whatever is happening. A special awareness is called for.

Even if harsh interventions succeed brilliantly, there is no cause for celebration. There has been injury. Someone's process has been violated.

Later on, the person whose process has been violated may well become less open and more defended. There will be a deeper resistance and possibly even resentment.

Making people do what you think they ought to do does not lead toward clarity and (quality) consciousness. While they may do what you tell them to do at the time, they will cringe inwardly, grow confused, and plot revenge.

That is why your victory is actually a failure.

To reinforce this culture of a process control environment and to seed these concepts that might seem strange or esoteric to a varied audience, we created a process tour of our operations for all of our associates. It began in 1992, and we called it "Sys-Tao."

Every Tuesday for more than twelve years, we assembled about 25 associates from cross-functional departments, disparate geographical areas, and every level of the organization. The group always included both new hires and veterans, and the idea was that every associate would participate one time every year.

The "Sys" stands for the System. It refers to *systems thinking*. It is *all* the blue boxes added together and managed by our associates to form a single holistic process. Its aim is to "quench the thirst of our customer's customer."

"Tao," on the other hand, has to do with the green arrows, the caring relationships, the customer focus, and the quality consciousness that allows the total system to always become better. It refers to *understanding relationships*. Tao, as in Taoism, is a pretty big subject unto itself, but, in a concise way, it conjures up all of the distinctions found in Asian cultures.

"Sys-Tao," therefore, is mysterious yet apparent, paradoxical yet sensible. It rhetorically acknowledges that we live to become better and suggests the *way* of continual improvement for all relationships — between departments, functions, locations, levels, bosses, workers, external suppliers and customers, and even shareholders.

Sys-Tao participants gathered around a huge round conference table, which by its physical presence symbolically shouted equality and collaboration among all in attendance. Our purpose was always the same. Using the kaizen model as a map, you could figuratively "**S**taple **Y**our**S**elf **T**o **A**n **O**rder," go with the flow, and follow the lifecycle of a perfect Coke. So, in this way, Sys-Tao also became a useful acronym suggesting *flow*.

Because the group was so diverse, each person present was by definition the resident expert for some part of the process. Associates were randomly asked to introduce themselves and explain how they fit into the flow of this model.

They were encouraged to talk about things gone wrong – TGWs:

TGWs are the raw materials for improving the process.

Blame was always discouraged, and collaboration regarding what could be a way to improve the process was always encouraged:

Failure is not fatal, and success is not final.
Our purpose is simply to become better.

Most problems were conflicts with another department. Typically, another participant representing that function, along with others around the table with relevant knowledge, would begin to speak up — but not before their obligatory introduction and explanation of how they too fit into this holistic system.

These discussions illustrated why it is best "when delicate facilitations far outnumber harsh interventions." A typical conflict between warehouse workers and truck drivers deals with the differences between *road worthy*, and *driver friendly*. The permutations and combinations of the mix of hundreds of constantly changing products and packages that must be picked from inventory and bundled for each customer's specific *drop* is a daunting task and a moving target. "Road worthy," of course, means that each customer's drop must fit on the truck and not tip over en route. "Driver friendly," on the other hand means that they must be easy to handle for the drivers/merchandisers. Sounds simple enough, but without constant collaboration, trends in the everyday course of events make yesterday's best practices into tomorrow's harsh interventions.

In 1993, to further illustrate this collaborative process control environment, we even made a video, *Sys-Tao the Movie*. Like all great movies, (we thought it was pretty good), it was followed two years later by a sequel, *The Sys-Tao Experience*. Then, to celebrate our family's 75th anniversary in the business, we did it again. This time we called it *A Family Tradition since 1922*.

Each of these videos emphasizes the principles and the process that are the subject of this chapter, and they were always an integral part of our weekly meetings. To see them, just visit Sys-Tao.org/links.

It is my belief that a corporate culture like this can evolve only when it is helped along by management's constant nurturing of these relationships with "just-like" references and metaphors in order to replace old habits.

The principles of Sys-Tao were also captured in a white paper that was handed out at every Sys-Tao meeting, along with a commemorative perfect bottle of Coke with the word Sys-Tao emblazoned upon it.

The Sys-Tao bottle soon took on a life of its own. It was never sold in the commercial market, but every week for more than a decade these bottles were handed out only to the attendees of our Sys-Tao meetings. As our world-class reputation grew, bottlers from all over the world began to request invitations to these meetings. At last count, representatives from well over 100 bottling operations from more than 25 countries had visited our company.

And guess what? These bottles became one of the most collectable of all Coke bottles ever. Just Google: "eBay Sys-Tao." These bottles have sold for hundreds of dollars at auction, and they remain a sought-after collector's item.

"Constancy of purpose" was Deming's first principle, and all of these examples are tangible testimony that we always adhered to the same principles and the steadfast commitment to always improve the process.

The Sys-Tao White Paper that was handed out at these meetings is reprinted in the following chapter. Please keep in mind, as you read this material, that it was not altered for the purposes of this book, and that it was originally intended only for our Great Plains associates. As a result, it contains some company-specific language (jargon) and graphics that are not at first clear to the uninitiated, but I believe it is more valuable in this way, because it gives you, the reader, another example — just like the Sys-Tao movies — of the ways we shared and acted out our transformational journey together.

Frankly, it is a difficult read because, while explaining the blue boxes and the green arrows and the differences in our cultures (the cowboys and the Indians), many of the metaphors are drawn directly from the *Tao Te Ching*. And of course, this white paper was not just handed out to our associates; it was a reference guide for dialogue, conversation, and collaboration in our seminar-style meetings. As such, it is a deeply layered document — an artifact of the cultural change that we were able to achieve together.

Hopefully, you will read and re-read it at your leisure.

CHAPTER TEN

Sys-Tao™

Staple **Y**our **Self T**o **A**n **O**rder

&

Go with the Flow

Most Westerners are analytical and pragmatic by nature. A System, "Sys," to us is the sum of many separate parts; many functional details which when added together accomplish a purpose. We are specialists by training. We take pride in knowing our part and doing our job. For us, reality is in the results. Coke is it. It's the Real Thing! Always Coca-Cola!

According to the Chinese, the ultimate essence of reality is "Tao." The principle characteristic of Tao is the cyclical nature of its ceaseless motion; all developments in nature—those in the physical world as well as those in the psychological and social realms—show cyclical patterns. For them, reality is invisible. Reality is the process.

This idea of cyclical patterns between the limits of two polar opposites is what they refer to as "Yin" and "Yang," the Yang having reached its climax retreats in favor of the Yin, the Yin having reached its climax, retreats in favor of the Yang. According to the Chinese, we must *go with the flow.*

This is not unlike the Deming cycle of "Plan, Do, Study, Act." "Plan" and "Do" are similar to the Yang, while "Study" and "Act" are more like the Yin. Yang is the more physically active concept –not unlike our Western point of view, the real world of analytical work—"What is." Yin is the more passive concept—more like the world of holistic meditation and contemplation—*"What Could Be."*

The Process of Continual Improvement
Moving "what is" to "what could be"

A PROCESS THAT TALKS TO ITSELF

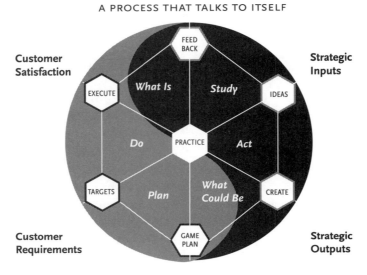

THE PROCESS PLAYBOOK

All manifestations of Tao are generated by the dynamic interplay of these two polar ideas. Westerners have difficulty understanding that these conceptual opposites do not belong to separated "independent functional" categories but are extreme poles of a single "interdependent cross-functional" whole. Nothing is either only Yin or only Yang. Everything is relationships. All natural phenomena are manifestations of the continuous oscillation between both poles. The natural order is the dynamic balance between both Yin and Yang. Deming would call understanding of this holistic point of view Profound Knowledge.

Change is natural and continual. Change, in this view, does not occur as a consequence of some force but is a natural tendency, innate in all things and situations. The universe is engaged in ceaseless motion and activity, in intimate interrelationships in a continual cosmic process of creation. According to an ancient text, "*Tao* is—the *Way.*"

> Tao means how: how things happen, how things work. Tao is the single principle underlying all creation. Tao is the way.
>
> Tao cannot be defined, because it applies to everything. You cannot define something in terms of itself. If you can define a principle it is not Tao.

Tao is a principle. Creation, on the other hand, is a process. That is all there is; principle and process, how and what.

All creation unfolds according to Tao. There is no other way. Tao cannot be defined, but Tao can be known. The method is meditation, or being aware of what is happening. By being aware of what is happening, I begin to sense how it is happening. I begin to sense Tao.

To become aware of what is happening I must set aside my personal prejudices or bias. Prejudiced people see only what fits those prejudices.

The method of meditation works because principle and process are inseparable. All process reveals the underlying principle. This means that I can know Tao. I can know the way.

By knowing Tao, I know how things happen.

Great Plains is a System. We are all a Chain of Customers. The creative process of Continual Improvement of our System and strengthening this Chain depends on how well we know the way. "*Kaizen*" is the Japanese word for Continual Improvement of a system. "*Tao*" is the way.

Sys-Tao implies both "What" and "How." It implies profound knowledge of our entire process. The Goal of our System is never ending. It is the Continual Improvement of the process of Continuous Customer Service. In order to improve our System we must know how. We must know the way.

The Process of Continual Improvement

The way of our Customers is the way of an order. If you will symbolically **S**taple **Y**our **S**elf **T**o **A**n **O**rder, you will quite literally *go with the flow*, and you will find yourself on a tour of our Great Plains System. You will experience *"The Way It Is."* If you allow yourself the opportunity to meditate you will better know how things really happen. You will come to know *"The Way It Could Be."* This is our Goal— "To continually improve our Process of Continuous Customer Service."

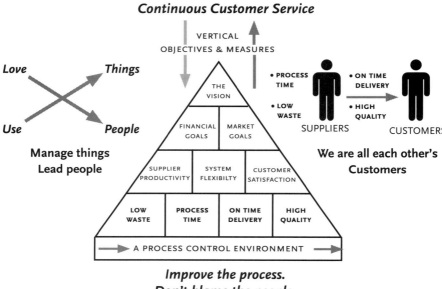

Improve the process.
Don't blame the people.

Process Capabilities must Continually Improve if they are always to exceed forever increasing Customer Requirements. To know the way, we must be aware of both the "Voice of the Process," and the Voice of the Customer." The Voice of the Process can be measured in terms of "Process Time" and "Waste." The Voice of the Customer can be measured in terms of "On Time" and "Quality."

As these measures improve we will approach our goal. In order for these measures to improve we must know the way. We must have profound knowledge of the entire process—an interdependent and universal system in dynamic balance that includes both Customers and Suppliers.

Whenever we make decisions; whenever we act; we are never just "doing;" we are always "becoming." Life is change. Growth is optional. We must choose wisely. As our systems become more precise, our relationships will become more intimate; as our relationships become more intimate our systems will become more precise. We will become better.

This is how our visions become shared. First, we decide for ourselves. We start by pursuing our own personal vision, but as we learn to listen carefully to the vision of others, we see that our vision is part of something larger. This does not diminish our sense of responsibility for the vision. It deepens it, and our stewardship for the vision is what allows us to change our paradigm. The vision ceases to be a possession as in "this is my vision. "Instead, it becomes "our calling."

According to George Bernard Shaw, "This is the true joy of life . . . being used for a purpose recognized by yourself as a mighty one . . . being a force of nature instead of a feverish, selfish little clod of ailments and grievances complaining that the world will not devote itself to making you happy."

> The master in the art of living makes little distinction between his work and his play, his labor and his leisure, his mind and his body, his education and his recreation, his love and his religion. He hardly knows which is which. He simply pursues his vision of excellence in whatever he does, leaving others to decide whether he is working or playing. To him he is always doing both.
>
> — ZEN BUDDHIST TEXT

A journey of a thousand miles begins with a single step.

Staple **Y**our **S**elf **T**o **A**n **O**rder & Enjoy Coca-Cola.

Our purpose is to provide Continuous Customer Service. To do this, we must Continually Improve both our vision of "*What Could Be*," as well as our understanding of "*What Is*." Continual Improvement is a journey, and both "*What Is*" and "*What Could Be*" are moving along together with us.

Our system is made up of many parts, and we are each accountable for different types of functional expertise. Everyone's understanding of the big picture is essential for our success and happiness along the way.

Every journey requires a map. Our company is held together by the shared vision of our Customer-Focused Processes and Strategies. To the extent that we have profound knowledge of these Processes and Strategies, we have a map. We know "*What Is*." As we improve our Process we gain insight towards improving our Strategies and vice versa. As we improve "*What Is*" we gain profound knowledge of "*What Could Be*." We learn, we grow, and we continually improve together.

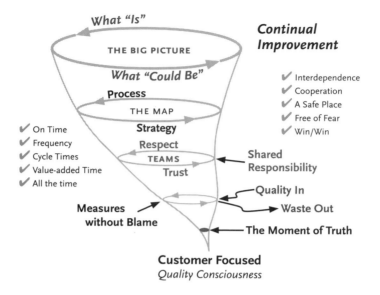

Despite our functional expertise, we can never be successful or happy unless we work together as a Team. Teamwork requires Mutual Trust and Respect for everything and everyone. We must share the responsibility and work together inside the Process and through the Strategy. All things are interdependent and we must always cooperate and strive for Win/Win relationships with Customers and Suppliers and with our fellow associates—both internal and external—to our Company.

Growing, Learning, and Improving comes from within and, of course, results must come later. As on any journey, it would be foolish to look only in the rear view mirror. We must look inward—not backward—in order to go forward. As we improve our Process, we will put "Quality" in, and we take "Waste" out of everything we do. Naturally then, these are the things to measure.

Finally, Quality is added only when it means something of value for our External Customers, and if it does not add Value for the External Customer, then it must be Waste. When our Team efforts are focused at the Moment of Truth for our Customers, everything we do naturally improves and the power of this force pulls us forward towards "What Could Be." We all become better.

PART THREE

The Principles

*I*t is time to answer the question:

How can we reconcile the paradox of a mission statement that requires satisfaction and happiness for customers as well as financial success for the company and its shareholders?

The Time Paradigm

T hruput is good for everyone. We know that thruput is a good thing for shareholders, because it is "the money coming in" to the company. Likewise, thruput over time is also a good thing for customers, because it is an objective measure of *customer value*, and it enables management to better focus on *quality consciousness* (solving customer problems and achieving customer satisfaction and happiness). Increasing thruput is always a good thing. There is no paradox regarding thruput. It is an easy concept to understand, to embrace, and to implement. Maximizing thruput over time (thruput per hour) is always good for everyone.

There are only three kinds of money: money coming in, money going out, and money stuck inside.

Total Operating Expense has been defined as "the money going out" of a company. It is the total cash operating cost of the system (the process). And then there is "the money stuck inside," the *Capital Costs*. These costs that are either "going out" or are "stuck inside" must represent 100% of the paradox.

Unfortunately, accounting can't distinguish the difference between the good costs (*capability*) that add *customer value* and the bad costs (*waste*) that do not. Clearly we should maximize the one and minimize the other. So how can we resolve this dilemma?

It is common sense that we must know our *costs*, but faced with this dilemma, it is no longer common sense that we should continue the practice of managing productivity based on either "cost per unit produced" or "cost per unit sold."

If we can't tell the difference between good costs and bad costs, what can these statistics possibly tell us? If one company added 5% in good costs, while another removed 5% in good costs, this cost per unit thinking would surely reward cost reduction and inhibit process improvement. Eventually, the company that added capability would do better than the company that reduced it. Cost per unit statistics might be predictive in the very short term, but clearly they are misleading over time.

The implications of this example are in conflict with the common practice of what I refer to as "the cost paradigm," which treats all cost reductions as a good thing. We need a different paradigm — one that will help us distinguish the good costs from the bad costs. I will call it "the time paradigm."

Simply stated, *the time paradigm* is made up of five "time" parameters that affect the process flow (thruput per hour) of the kaizen model:

- **frequency**
- **all the time**
- **cycle time**
- **on time**
- **value-added time**

These principles will be discussed in the following chapters. Taken together, they directly affect both *process capability* improvements and *process waste* reductions.

The time paradigm, therefore, addresses Deming's Point #5:

> Improve constantly and forever the system of production and service, to improve Quality and productivity (Capability), and thus constantly decrease costs (Waste).

But, will the *waste* reductions offset the cost of increasing *capability?* It is interesting that the cost paradigm is so strong that most people don't even bother to ask how *thruput* (the money coming in) or *capital costs* (the money "stuck inside") might be affected.

Most cost paradigm thinkers find it easier to focus on the cost of capability and not the potential for increased thruput. Remember, thruput is a much larger number than *gross profit*, and it is, therefore, more sensitive to changes in *volume* effected by increased *capability*. **Appendix II** — GAAP vs. Thruput Accounting — delves more deeply into this point.

It is also extremely counterintuitive and hard to comprehend that a change from the cost paradigm to the time paradigm will somehow reduce the need for *capital spending* — buying trucks and machinery, etc. — but, as we will see, that is also the case (*see* Chapter Eighteen . . . *Muri, Mura, Muda*).

Furthermore, reliance on the cost paradigm and failure to appreciate the time paradigm can result in decisions that will needlessly increase capital spending and restrict thruput (*see* Chapter Twenty . . . *The Goldratt Shirt Factory*).

When taken together, these five parameters also provide insight into *understanding variation* (*see* Chapter Fifteen . . . *Understanding Variation*).

Without a different paradigm, continued focus on "cost" runs the risk of cutting *capability* along with *waste*, retarding *thruput*, and increasing dependence on *capital spending*.

Finally, and importantly, the time paradigm resolves the paradox of a mission statement that focuses on customer satisfaction and happiness vs. the need for financial success for the company and its shareholders.

Let's begin with *Frequency*.

CHAPTER TWELVE

Frequency

Which Circle Are You Standing in?

T he next graphic poses a straightforward question that tugs at the paradox regarding customer satisfaction and happiness vs. the need for financial success for the company and its shareholders. It implies that you can deliver truckload quantities when needed on one extreme, or frequent and consistent delivery of much smaller quantities (drop sizes) on the other.

Frequency x Drop Size = Volume

What happens to volume if **Frequency** changes or varies?

If you stand in the company circle, your mind might focus on cost, and you'd favor large drop sizes. If, on the other hand, you take the customer circle point of view, you would probably prefer higher and more consistent service frequencies, because it would reduce waste and improve the capability to increase volume. Intuitively, you know the customer is right, but your traditional cost accounting paradigms pull you back to the company circle.

Looked at this way, frequency and drop size are the flip sides of the same coin, because if we doubled our drop size and halved our frequency you could argue that, mathematically, volume would remain unchanged.

What we really want is to have volume increase, because volume drives thruput, and thruput is good for everyone. So, what actually happens when we reduce frequency and increase drop size? If you say it doesn't matter, you are hopelessly trapped in *the cost paradigm*.

When we reduce frequency, "out of stocks" increase, "out of dates" increase, back rooms become overstocked, "breakage, damaged & lost" increases, order accuracy decreases, caring relationships become strained, customer satisfaction diminishes, and, oh yeah, volume & thruput decline. If we let frequency vary in order to "optimize" the drop size, customer satisfaction surely suffers. Should we have minimum drop sizes or minimum service levels? What is an "optimum" drop size? Which circle are you standing in?

There is another subtler and more important aspect of the relationship between frequency and drop size. In the real world, all statistics fluctuate around the average.

If a customer averages 210 cases per week and gets daily service, that works out to an average of 30 cases per day (210 divided by seven days) plus or minus a few cases for normal fluctuations (10% in this example). Now, if we apply the "more efficient" larger drop size thinking, and cut service frequency to once a week, the drop size will increase to 210, but the 10% normal fluctuation increases to plus or minus 21 cases — a potential swing of 42 cases! During periods of promotional pricing, the swings in volume could become violent, and it will be a week before mistakes can be corrected — unless, of course, we schedule special off-frequency deliveries. Variations like this can cause the kaizen model to literally shake. On the other hand, with more frequent deliveries the variation in this example is reduced to just three cases and mistakes can be corrected daily.

These important relationships are illustrated below:

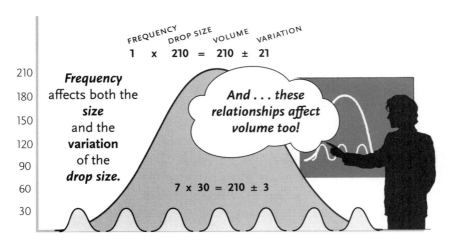

There's more. When you look again at the kaizen model, it is clear that these frequency/drop size relationships apply to all the green arrows between every blue box, and between all the internal customers — not just between one company and its external customers.

There are kaizen-like molecules nested in every blue box of the kaizen model, just as there are more kaizen models making up the chain of customers often referred to as the *Supply Chain*, as shown below. We prefer to call it the *Demand Chain*, because it puts the emphasis on the customer circle. It is a matter of how you look at it, but whatever you call it, the frequency/drop size relationships are very important and they have a lot to do with your own point of view.

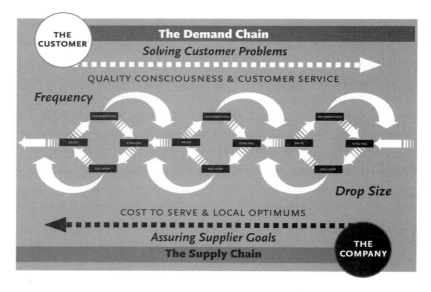

All processes are just a long string of kaizen molecules. How you manage them depends on which circle you find yourself standing in.

When managers focus attention on their own blue box, they naturally focus on "efficient batch sizes," and feel the necessity of managing their people with incentives to make their blue box more productive. They literally push products down the supply chain. Terms like "cases per truck" and "cost to serve" slip into the lexicon. Some "cost" accounting professionals refer to this as "activity-based costing" (*see* **Appendix II** . . . GAAP vs. Thruput Accounting). Unfortunately, these cost allocations focus even more attention on local optimums, which in turn harm relationships and deny the next blue box some amount of customer satisfaction.

On the flip side, when managers take a more holistic view, and allow their associates to provide adequate service frequency, relationships improve, customer focus increases, and quality consciousness becomes the norm. Customers are enabled to pull products along the demand chain as needed, and the whole system becomes better. Continual improvement becomes the culture, and not just the name for a project.[1]

When this happens, managers become leaders and associates become empowered to manage the process. Deming would call this "instituting leadership."

There is, of course, far more to *the time paradigm* than the frequency/drop size relationship. In the next chapter we will cover three more of these important parameters.

---

1 A rather famous Hewlett-Packard video illustrates via a skit just what happens when management shifts its focus from pushing products down the Supply Chain to customers vs. a focus that allows customers to pull products along the Demand Chain as they are needed. This skit is linked at Sys-Tao.org/links.

CHAPTER THIRTEEN

All the Time, Cycle Time, & On Time

Consumers, shoppers, and retail customers don't stop on Saturdays and Sundays or at night, so why should we, or any other supplier in this chain of customers, just stop? After all, our kaizen model is a biological metaphor — it must be lifelike, and it can't just quit breathing or shut its heart down for weekends. Unless things go on normally around the clock and around the calendar, our systems will suffer.

In the next illustration, a student of *the time paradigm* has reviewed the fact that increasing frequency reduces the variation in drop sizes.

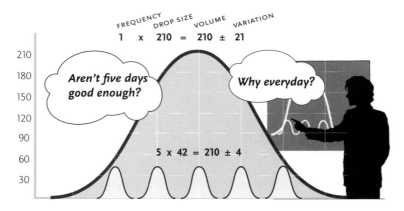

He is beginning to understand that keeping the process going *All the Time* also reduces fluctuations. For instance, the drop sizes become both larger and more unpredictable on Mondays and Fridays if the process shuts down for weekends as shown below:

EVERYDAY SERVICE WOULD EVEN OUT THE FLOW

When any blue box stops processing, it throws both surges and fluctuations into the system that in turn disrupt the overall flow. It's just like when we allow service frequencies to vary. Retailers are forced to stock up, causing abnormally large fluctuations in inventory. It is the beginning of a system-generated vicious circle.

Subconsciously, this might remind the student of his rush hour commute to and from work, the stop and go traffic jams, and his related stress along the way. He realizes that these fluctuations don't average out; they accumulate!

And, it occurs to him that *cycle time*, the time it takes to go around the kaizen model, also affects process flow — process capability and process waste. For instance, order accuracy is affected by excessive cycle times. Ordering for the weekend is really just a guess, "just in case." The shorter the cycle time is, the more accurate the order will be. As this rhythm quickens and smooths out, so does the process.

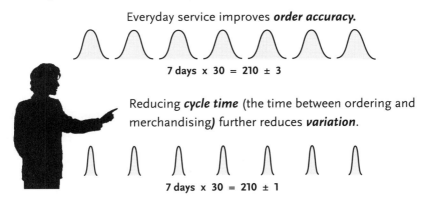

Everyday service improves **order accuracy.**

7 days x 30 = 210 ± 3

Reducing **cycle time** (the time between ordering and merchandising*)* further reduces **variation**.

7 days x 30 = 210 ± 1

Thinking in this way, he wonders why electronic orders moving across the top of the kaizen model often seem to move even slower than the trucks moving down the highway on the bottom of the model. Why does it sometimes take 48 hours to deliver something less than a few hours away? It is as if some *blue box* manager were standing in the *company circle*, batching and staging the orders for processing at his own convenience and without concern for the overall process flow. Why is this so often the case? Why do local optimums so often win out over holistic points of view?

When this happens, it affects the cycle time of the entire process. It starves the blue boxes downstream. Without work to process, they become serious bottlenecks to the overall system's capability.

And then, when the upstream blue boxes suddenly release large batches to the downstream constraints, it builds excessive inventory that could have been processed sooner while the constraint was sitting idle. Is this not waste too?

For instance, entire fleets of trucks often sit idle overnight and on weekends waiting for tomorrow's loads or Monday's surge. As a result, these fleets are often *more than twice the size they need be.*

Finally, he realizes that variation in drop sizes could also affect being *on time.* Here, on time clearly implies the same time every time, because that is what customers want. And, if we aren't on time for one customer, how can we be on time for the next customer? After all, these fluctuations don't average out; they accumulate!

Variation of **drop size** also affects being
on time!

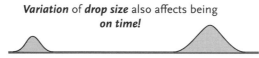

So, not being on time is like a multiplier of waste. The more one blue box runs behind, the more all the other blue boxes get behind too. Some of the effects of not being on time are summarized in the next graphic. Here, the blue boxes are external customers served by any delivery system, but it applies to internal customers in the same way.

How does **not** being **On Time** affect things like . . .

• missed appointments	• refused orders
• over-time	• cycle time
• off frequency	• off sequence
• order accuracy	• returned goods
• out of stock	• out of date
• equipment required	• staffing levels

And **how** do these things affect . . .

• Thruput	• Capital Expenditures
• Total Operating Expenses	• Cash Operating Profit

Keeping the process going, both around the clock and around the calendar, at a high frequency and with short cycle times will clearly increase process capability and decrease waste. Customer service — including being on time — will improve, and thruput will improve. The kaizen model will quit shaking, and instead it will more likely "hum in perfect harmony."

But then, as we shall see in the next chapter, sometimes it is best to just take time out.

CHAPTER FOURTEEN

Value–Added Time

A journey of a thousand miles begins with a single step.

— Lao Tzu

But why so many steps?

— Bob Browne

Every blue box has a cost, and every blue box takes time. If the time adds value for the customer, it is *value-added time* (VAT) and the cost is *capability*. If the time does not add value for the customer, it is *non-value-added time* (NVAT) and the cost is *waste*.

Consider the 17 value-added blue boxes as shown in the *Demand Chain Model*. If the output of each of them were 99% perfect, then the output (sometimes called "first-run yield") of this 17-step process would be just 84% ($99\%^{17steps}=84\%$). It would fail 16% of the time!

A Chain of Customers

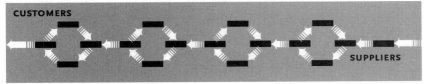

Even if the 17 blue boxes were 99% perfect, the process would fail 16% of the time!

Clearly 99% is not good enough, and obviously the implication of more blue boxes, especially if some are non-value-added, is enormous. There are literally hundreds of blue boxes in most demand chains, because there are more kaizen-like molecules nested in every blue box of the kaizen model.

If the process described above had a more realistic 170 steps, and if each step were ten times more precise — 99.9% perfect — the outcome would be unchanged ($99.9\%^{170steps}=84\%$). Intuitively, we should realize that it is easier to eliminate non-value-added time steps than it is to continually strive for more precision in every step.

In other words, "doing the wrong things righter" is not a good strategy for improving the process.

It is unfortunate that our accounting systems can't distinguish good costs from bad costs, but both value-added time and non-value-added time are always obvious to the customer's customer, and non-value-added time is *waste* that could be eliminated.

This is another reason why the green arrow relationships between the blue boxes are more important than the precision of a single blue box. If the box doesn't add value, don't improve it. Get rid of it! Don't confuse efficiency with unnecessary activity. An unnecessary activity, even if performed perfectly, is still waste.

Likewise, increasing the capacity of an upstream blue box whose capacity already exceeds a downstream blue box will do nothing to increase the system's thruput per hour. Improving the capacity of the constraint, the bottleneck, will help, but eliminating non-value-added time or allowing the constraint to add value more of the time, "24/7/365," will likely help more, and it is easier to do.

Examples of this surround us and are taken for granted. Not so long ago ships were loaded with cargo nets and then unloaded onto trucks, which were then unloaded and reloaded onto trains that transported the goods to more trucks. Improving the design of the cargo net, or trying to minimize load/unload time would have been a tempting way of improving the system. But of course, there was a better way that got rid of these steps altogether. Today, containerized freight is more than a way of life — it is an industry of its own, created by the elimination of non-value-added time. In a similar way, streaming media is now starting to replace DVDs and broadcast television. What's next? That is for you to decide.

This idea holds true in any organization, on any scale. No matter how small, *non-value-added time* is *non-value-added time* — and *improved* non-value-added time is *still* non-value-added time! If it can be eliminated, it should be. Anywhere you see inventory is a good place to look for non-value-added time. If the process is not flowing evenly around the clock and around the calendar, there is non-value-added time somewhere nearby.

The kaizen model represents "just in time" process flow, and it is a customer-focused philosophy whose primary objective is the elimination of waste. Waste is understood to be anything other than the minimum amount of equipment, inventory, labor, space, and time which are absolutely essential to add *Customer Value*. By definition, non-value-added time blue boxes are *waste*.

When all associates work together to eliminate non-value-adding jobs, the overall process naturally improves, but job security takes on new meaning. Is this not another paradox?

We all want to become better, but no one wants to lose his job. Cutting jobs shuts down intrinsic motivation and disables a *Process Control Environment*. Fear is reintroduced to the work force, trust is destroyed, process improvement slows down, and it is not long before silos reappear and the *Command and Control* ways of the past take over.

People are valuable. Non-value-added jobs are a waste. These distinctions must not be confused. At Great Plains it was essential that everyone understand that there was always an opportunity to improve their own self-worth by moving to a position that added more value. This is an important example of both how and why management must assure that caring relationships are always present — by respecting every associate and creating opportunities for them to improve their self-worth. Becoming better is everyone's job. Mutual respect for everyone builds trust and creates a culture of shared beliefs.

Deming's final two points emphasize the importance of these distinctions, and the resolution of this potential paradox:

> 13. Institute a vigorous program of education and self-improvement.

> 14. Put everybody in the company to work to accomplish the transformation. The transformation is everybody's job.

The past few chapters explained the five parameters that make up what I have called *the time paradigm*, and because each of these parameters deals with the idea of variation, we should spend a little more time on the subject of *variation*.

CHAPTER FIFTEEN

Understanding Variation

U nderstanding variation is closely related to the time paradigm:

- Frequency
- Cycle Time
- All the Time
- On Time
- Value-Added Time

Variation creates waste and reduces the capability to provide quality service. Reducing variation is, therefore, a very good thing.

The time paradigm (increasing frequency; reducing cycle time; operating consistently more of the time; being on time; while minimizing non-value-added time) shows us how to reduce variation. Furthermore, not being on time is like a multiplier; it is both a cause and an effect of variation.

In order to measure *Process Variation* within systems, Deming advocated *Statistical Process Control*. The mathematics are rigorous, and the management concepts associated with using SPC stand in stark contrast to the more traditional paradigms such as the "management by objectives" approach to getting results. Deming was also opposed to incentives, quotas, numerical goals, and inspections. No wonder most people don't know much about SPC.

Furthermore, old paradigms really do die hard. It is difficult to let go of traditional beliefs and change established habits. Why isn't a minimum *drop size* a good thing? Why shouldn't we give quantity discounts for truckload drop sizes? Doesn't it cost a lot more to operate 24/7/365 and to deliver more often? Won't the increased "cost to serve" outweigh any benefits? Higher frequency means more drops, so doesn't that mean more trucks? Everything is so counterintuitive.

So . . . let's slow down and begin thinking about variation from the very beginning.

For most people, our traditional beliefs regarding variation and averages were learned by flipping coins or rolling dice. For instance, rolling dice is all about the combinations and permutations of two six-sided cubes. Mathematicians refer to this as an example of the binomial distribution, but odds-makers and gamblers just know that there are 36 possible outcomes. There is just one way to get *snake eyes* (double ones) or *box cars* (double sixes) and there are six ways to *shoot craps* (get a seven), and that is the reason it is easier to roll craps than any other combination.

Now, if you are neither a mathematician nor a gambler, and you have no idea what this is about, suffice it to say that there is a distinct probability what you will get each time you roll the dice. For either snake eyes or boxcars there is just one chance in 36, but there are six chances in 36 that you will "crap out."

Statisticians tell us that as we roll the dice more and more times, the probability of craps or any other outcome gets closer and closer to what is called a *Normal (probability) Distribution* curve. Taken together, it can be illustrated like this:

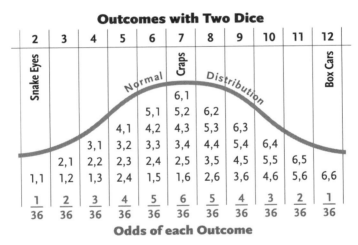

Deming suggested that we should measure the natural variation of the outcomes of a process and then calculate the spread of the bell-shaped curve in order to determine whether the process has the capability to perform within a customer's expectations (specification limits). Because we can know the spread of the bell-shaped curve, we can also know the probability that the process will fail to meet the customers' expectations. This is what he referred to as Statistical Process Control (SPC).

For instance, if, as shown below, we flipped coins instead of rolling dice, and gave *heads* a value of six and *tails* a value of eight, it is clear that after many tosses, the average value would again be seven.

Outcomes with One Coin

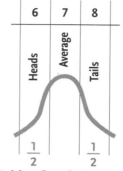

Odds of each Outcome

The variation from the average for flipping one coin is plus or minus one, which is far less than the variation of plus or minus five for the dice rolls. Said in SPC lingo, as the bell shaped curve flattens, variation increases, and the process becomes less capable, but, in either case, the results are always predictable.

If the customer's specification limits were seven plus or minus one, the "coin flip" process would have the capability to meet these requirements 100% of the time. The "dice roll" process, on the other hand, would fall outside the customer's specification limits 56% (20/36) of the time.

From our Coke truck example, we know that doubling the frequency cuts the drop size in half, but because we are going twice as often, the thruput over time stays the same and the variation is cut in half. If we measured the variation of the drop size using Deming's methods it would look something like the next illustration of "Statistical Process Control (SPC) Run Charts:"

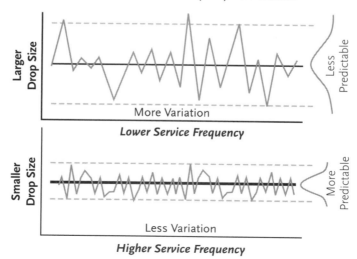

Lower Service Frequency

Higher Service Frequency

Statistically, the dashed lines, referred to as *Control Limits*, represent three standard deviations on either side of the average drop size (the solid line).

These control limits are not set by management; they are instead a measure of the system's own inherent variation. Reducing this variation is dependent upon improving the process, and that brings us full circle back to the time paradigm.

The mathematics and big words associated with SPC are challenging, but the takeaway is that we can be sure with 99.6% confidence that these processes will perform inside the process control limits (a six sigma spread about the average) which is derived from the process' own data as shown below.

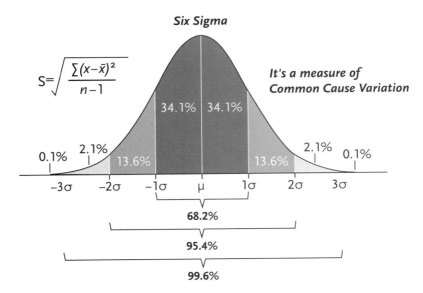

Six Sigma

$$S=\sqrt{\frac{\Sigma(x-\bar{x})^2}{n-1}}$$

It's a measure of Common Cause Variation

34.1%   34.1%

0.1%   2.1%   13.6%   13.6%   2.1%   0.1%

−3σ   −2σ   −1σ   μ   1σ   2σ   3σ

68.2%

95.4%

99.6%

Deming called this variation "common cause," because it is the result of unknown random factors inherent in the process itself. He would describe drop sizes outside these statistically calculated control limits as "special cause" variations, because they are more than likely known, non-random, and often extraneous to the process itself. For instance, a change in pricing would surely create special cause variations.

In this way, increasing frequency (as well as improving any of the other time paradigm parameters) reduces common cause variation, and increases the process capability to meet or exceed a customer's expectations (the capability to operate within the customer's specification limits).

Statistical process control is *not* an objective measure of product quality; it *is* an objective measure of process capability to predictably deliver quality. Quality, after all, is a subjective characteristic that resides in the eye of the beholder, namely inside the customer's specification limits. It is everyone's job to be quality conscious in everything we do and to develop process capabilities that can deliver the quality that each customer desires.

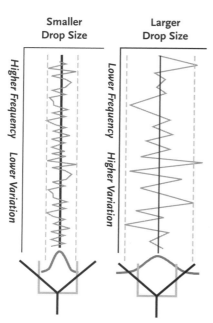

In this illustration, the SPC Run Charts have been rotated 90 degrees, and I have included our "Japanese goal posts" at the bottom in order to illustrate what is most desirable. The customer's "specification limits" (the traditional goal posts), must not be confused with the "process control limits" (the dashed lines). The one measures the customer's minimum requirements while the other measures the inherent process capability (common cause variation). As you can see, the higher-frequency system can more predictably deliver quality service.

Eastern cultures have always understood that "reality is in the process," a difficult concept for most westerners, who believe that "reality is in the results." You can't improve results, but you can always improve a process.

Aristotle had said, " We are what we repeatedly do; excellence then, is not an act, but a habit." Then, someone else said, "Practice makes perfect." I say, "Practice makes us lucky" . . . our process becomes more predictable when we remove common cause variation . . . Aristotle was right; Deming just figured out how to measure it.

Goldratt wrote about yet another aspect of variation. He called it "the accumulation of fluctuations about dependent events," suggesting the counterintuitive idea that process variations don't average out. They, in fact, accumulate just like the rush hour traffic jams discussed earlier.

Each time you roll the dice, it is an "independent event," because no matter what you got on the last roll, it will have no effect on the next roll. So, if you roll the dice lots of times, the variations will average out to seven, because the outcomes are *independent* of each other. All this is intuitive and it creates the prevailing paradigm regarding system variation. Most people believe that variations within systems average out just like they do in Las Vegas.

But, the blue boxes in the kaizen model are not *independent* events. Each blue box is *dependent* on the one that comes before. According to Goldratt, variations between *dependent* events don't average out; they accumulate. That is why not being on time is a multiplier; it is both a cause and an effect of variation.

This "accumulation of (common cause) fluctuations about dependent events" creates a *supply chain* stack-up effect that is explained in Chapter Sixteen . . . *Second Semester Variation*.

Then in Chapter Seventeen . . . *Snap the Whip*, the inter-reactions between this supply chain effect and the effects of special cause variations going up the *demand chain* will be explained.

Does your hair hurt yet? . . . Read on.

Second Semester Variation . . .
Inventory is Time, Too

Consider the two-step process shown below. Each individual step has a *Cycle Time* of 24 hours, and the process runs "7/24/365." Each step has the capability to produce a batch of 4 units *without* variation — each step has a first-run yield of 100%. The process can, therefore, produce 4 units per batch with no inventory between the steps. The cycle time for the entire process is two days, because that is how long it takes raw materials to become finished goods. Likewise, there are 4 units of inventory inside each process step. In this way, inventory is time, too. There is, however, no inventory stacked up between the steps, because there is no variation.

A Two Step Process
***without* VARIATION**

CAPABILITY = 4 units

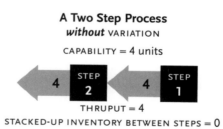

THRUPUT = 4
STACKED-UP INVENTORY BETWEEN STEPS = 0

Now consider the same process *with* common cause variation. This time let's assume that the process has the capacity to ship 5 units, but because of the variation there is an equal probability of either 3 or 5 units per batch, so the *average* capability is still 4 units. For instance, this could happen if the first-run yield periodically slips below 100%.

Careful study of the next process diagram shows that there are four permutations of thruput possibilities: (3,3), (3,5), (5,3), (5,5). Three of these yield a thruput of 3, and one yields a thruput of 5, so the average thruput is just 3.5 (3+3+3+5=14 divided by 4 permutations = 3.5). Furthermore, one combination, (5,3), results in the need to hold 2 additional units of inventory between the steps.

A Two Step Process
with VARIATION

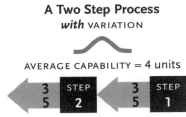

AVERAGE CAPABILITY = 4 units

THRUPUT = 3.5

STACKED-UP INVENTORY BETWEEN STEPS = 2

Variation has reduced thruput, and it has created waste in the form of unnecessary inventory (additional money stuck inside). Worse still, cycle time is now 2½ days because of the additional ½ day of inventory stacked up between the steps.

If we add more variation, as shown in the next illustration, thruput is further reduced, six units of waste is created (1½ days of inventory is stacked up between the steps), and the cycle time becomes 3½ days.

A Two Step Process
with *a lot* of VARIATION

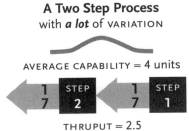

AVERAGE CAPABILITY = 4 units

THRUPUT = 2.5

STACKED-UP INVENTORY BETWEEN STEPS = 6

Adding steps makes the math harder, but the results get predictably worse. Adding just one step to this last example doubles the stacked-up inventory, the cycle time becomes 6 days (3 days in-process and 3 days stacked-up), and thruput dips to 1.75, because there are now eight permutations and only one of them yields a thruput of 7. The other seven permutations yield a thruput of just 1. So, on average, thruput is only 1.75 (1+1+1+1+1+1+7=14 divided by 8 = 1.75), as shown below.

A Three Step Process
with *a lot* of VARIATION

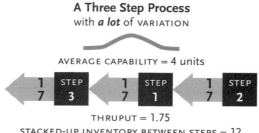

AVERAGE CAPABILITY = 4 units

THRUPUT = 1.75
STACKED-UP INVENTORY BETWEEN STEPS = 12

To be fair, as the inventory and cycle time stacks up, the thruput will approach 4 in each of these examples. Theoretically it will never quite reach 4, but it will continue to approach that limit.

Inventory and cycle time, on the other hand, will continue to stack up and accumulate. It will not average out or reach a limit; it will keep on growing forever! Of course, this excess inventory must be dealt with. We will deal with it in the next chapter.

But first, how might the application of "economies of scale" effect this situation? What would happen if the capability on one of these upstream process steps were to increase? For instance, what would happen if the capacity of the first step (the one on the right) were to double (e.g. 8 units with proportionate variation of either 2 or 14 units)?

Unfortunately, because of the downstream bottleneck(s), the system's process capability would not increase. Instead, inventory would just stack up behind the first bottleneck and cycle time would continue to grow. Don't confuse *capacity* with *capability*.

If the increased capacity were run just half the time, in order to compensate for this "stack-up" of inventory, it would effectively starve the constraints with too little inventory or flood them with too much. The cost of adding the increased capacity would be for naught. The only tangible result would be more inventory and increased cycle time.

In these examples, there are two ways to reduce inventory: Reduce the number of steps and/or reduce the variation. Adding capacity upstream of bottlenecks only adds inventory. It does not add process capability, because thruput remains unchanged.

There is, however, one more way to reduce inventory: Decreasing the cycle time of a process step can reduce variation. If the cycle time of each process step were cut in half, frequency could be doubled without increasing capacity, and the resultant decrease in batch size would cut the system's inventory in half. It is good for everyone . . . well, almost everyone.

According to generally accepted accounting principles, reducing inventories reduces GAAP profits. This is because GAAP inventory is "burdened" with "allocated" costs (things like labor expense, utilities, and even non-cash things like depreciation) so when inventories increase, these cost allocations are deferred and GAAP profits increase. Likewise, reducing inventories reduces GAAP profits. This is not common sense, but it is common practice. It runs counter to efficient operating practices and decision-making.

You would never have run your lemonade stand based on these principles.

This common practice is considered proper for financial reporting because it *theoretically* matches revenues with expenses, and it is accepted on Wall Street for purposes of valuation of the overall business results. But, operationally, from a process point of view, and in the long run, increasing inventory is not a good thing for anyone . . . customers or shareholders. It is just another bad habit.

Thruput is net sales minus the "product costs" of a perfect Coke. Gross profit is net sales minus "cost of goods sold." The additional inventory costs that GAAP assigns to the cost of goods sold are just an allocation; the money has already left the company.

Furthermore, the cost to carry inventory (a.k.a. working capital) is not a critical issue; the real issue is that the company has foregone thruput, and the total system's cycle time has increased. For instance, in the last example 12 additional units of inventory are stacked up inside the system (an inventory of 12 divided by daily thruput of 4 equals 3 days) And, because this inventory will continue to grow, the total system's cycle time will increase by more than three days in order to *almost* restore *average* process capability. This money stacked up and growing inside the company, no matter how you define it, is not *working*. It is waste, and if it weren't for variation, we would not have it. It's not the *cost* to carry inventory that matters most; it's the *time* it takes that matters most. Inventory is time too!

And, as you will see in the next chapter, making adjustments for this excess accumulation of inventories can cause problems too.

CHAPTER SEVENTEEN

Snap the Whip

WINSLOW HOMER'S 1872 PAINTING

S nap the Whip, or Crack the Whip as it is more often called, is a simple outdoor children's game that involves physical coordination. One player, chosen as the "head" of the whip, runs around in random directions, with subsequent players holding on to the hand of the previous player. The entire "tail" of the whip moves in those directions, but with much more force toward the end of the tail. The longer the tail, the more the forces act on the last player, and the tighter they have to hold on.

This is not unlike the *Bullwhip Effect*, a term used to describe how demand variability increases as it moves up the *Demand Chain*. If you were to "staple yourself to an order" and follow it from that consumer whose thirst was most recently quenched all the way back to Coke's world headquarters in Atlanta, Georgia, you would notice that both the batch sizes and the cycle times increase each step along the way.

Consumers enjoy Cokes one drink at a time, shoppers buy them in 12 packs, the retail trade buys them in cases, bottlers produce batch sizes measured in pallets, and raw materials are most often shipped to the bottlers in truckload quantities. Consumers operate within an arm's length of desire, but as we move up the demand chain, the larger factories upstream require larger batch sizes and longer lead times.

The longer it takes to react to a change in demand, the heavier the reaction must be. It is as if small changes in consumer demand can result in large variations in orders placed further upstream. The Bullwhip Effect, therefore, increases with the longer lead times created by the larger batch sizes necessary to accommodate the upstream "economies of scale."

Goldratt illustrates this phenomenon in a video on *Thinking Globally* which you can find at Sys-Tao.org/links.

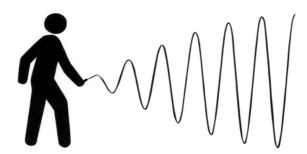

As explained in the last chapter, common cause variations coming down the supply chain will increase inventories. Increased inventory, of course, means even longer lead times. And, increasing capacity upstream of constrained resources (bottle necks) does not increase the system's capability; it just builds even more inventories and slows the system down even more.

The problems are, therefore, exacerbated when customers make (special cause) adjustments to compensate for these inventories that have accumulated as a result of (common cause) fluctuations along the supply chain. In fact, it causes the system to overreact in significant ways.

When these supplier-generated common cause variations coming down the supply chain collide with customer-generated special cause variations going up the demand chain, the Bullwhip Effect is further exacerbated.

Special cause variations occur whenever customers find it necessary to increase or decrease inventory levels. Suppliers are prone to misinterpret this as a change in consumer demand and a reason to adjust capacity. This, in turn, sets off a vicious circle of misinformation as inventory levels are adjusted and readjusted.

The reason for this misinterpretation is that most suppliers have no way to distinguish orders for the replenishment of a customer's thruput from orders for the adjustment of customer's inventory levels. Said another way, suppliers cannot distinguish pipeline fill from pipeline flow.

Dramatic changes in pricing, service frequencies, and cycle times are examples of operational reasons customers adjust inventories. Suppliers inflict common cause variation into the system via fluctuating first-run yields, excessive non-value-added steps, and not running consistently around the clock and around the calendar. Customers react to it by adjusting inventories, which introduces even more variation, and the system quickly spirals out of control.

The Bullwhip Effect has been acknowledged as a supply chain phenomenon since the 1960s, when the Sloan School of Management, Massachusetts Institute of Technology (MIT) developed a supply chain simulation known as "The Beer Game." This game simulates supply chain performance with one participant for each phase of the chain (consumer, retailer, distributor, brewery). The object of the game is to operate with as little total inventory as possible, and to avoid beer going "out of stock" at any level of the supply chain. The players can see each other's inventory, but they can't distinguish the differences in inventory changes and Thruput, and only one player knows what the market demand is at any given moment. Things tend to spiral out of control quickly as the various players react to what seem like wild and unexplainable swings in downstream ordering.

The game makes obvious what Winslow Homer illustrated nearly 100 years before. The beer game simulation is being played all over the world. Its effects are well known, but its resolution is not.

Furthermore, the beer game simulates only the Bull Whip effect, which results from customers changing inventory levels (special cause variations). It does not take into consideration the common cause variations discussed in the last chapter.

So, to recap: in the last two chapters, we've described two types of variation that affect the relationships between customers and suppliers:

1. *Common Cause Variations* going down the supply chain, from suppliers.

2. *Special Cause Variations* going up the demand chain, from customers.

When experienced together, they interact like colliding waves on the surface of a pond — they amplify one another and create *noise* in ways that are hard to measure or understand. Thought about in this way, it is easier to understand the dilemma caused by these combined disruptions, but the resolution of this dilemma is not yet clear — more about that later. The dilemma will be resolved when we consider *The Smart Order.*

But first, let's talk about three Japanese words, *Muri, Mura,* and *Muda* – and yet another aspect of the importance of embracing the time paradigm, and understanding variation.

CHAPTER EIGHTEEN

Muri, Mura, Muda

Loosely translated and taken together, these three Japanese words mean "waste." Together, they have been used often in the literature of "Just in Time" and "Lean Manufacturing," and they are attributed most often to Toyota's production system. Muri comes closer to our western understanding in that it refers to needless activities and wasted motions that overburden a system. *Mura* and *Muda*, on the other hand, are more difficult for the western mind to comprehend. Their definitions are closer to our ideas of "unevenness" and "excess."

What Deming taught was logical, but people tend to operate more analogically than logically, and the western mindset lacks rich analogies for what he was teaching. New ideas seem counterintuitive, without "just-like" references to help us understand and break old habits. We have few analogies for his logic, but the Japanese do.

The origin of these three words can be traced to the martial arts. The following anecdotal explanation of their etymology is reprinted from Rick Rowell's 2011 book, *Budo Theory: Exploring Martial Arts Practices:*

> While training in Japan one morning, in the *hombu dojo* (a Japanese term which literally means "place of the way," the formal gathering place for students of any Japanese martial arts style to conduct training), I was introduced to some terms that I had never heard before.
>
> While practicing *kihon* (a Japanese martial arts term meaning "basics") or *kata,* (detailed patterns of movements), Soke (the highest level leader of a school or style of martial art) would say "*Muda*" or "*Muri.*" I questioned Soke about this, but he only gave me a brief explanation. I think he just wanted me to keep punching during the morning workout.
>
> It was only later when I pinned him down after lunch that I got an explanation of what turned out to be everyday expressions in the Japanese language, "*Muri, Mura,* and *Muda,*" which helped me appreciate and understand my karate a little better.
>
> *Muri* means "no reason" or "no principle." It suggests that the *budoka* (a martial arts practitioner) should look at his technique to see

if it is beyond his current capabilities, and to search for the reason or principle behind the movement. Soke now only has to say, "*Muri*," and I understand that my movement has no meaning behind it or that it is currently beyond my capabilities.

Mura means "unnatural" or "inequality." This is the opposite of *Heijo* or "ordinary" (natural). *Mura* could refer to an unnatural movement, action or way of thinking. I realize that I have been punching unnaturally for 20 odd years now!

Muda refers to doing things in excess of what is needed, which could involve time, energy, length of the movement, etc. It was only when Soke got a Japanese dictionary and showed me the characters that I understood its meaning. *Muda* literally means "no horse." This doesn't mean that you don't have a horse, but that you have one and are not using it. It's like you are carrying a heavy bag on your shoulders while your horse walks beside you unburdened.

These three words give us a means to analyze our technique. If there is something wrong with our *kihon*, it   is usually for one of these reasons. So next time you are sweating in the *dojo* and just cannot figure out what is wrong, ask yourself if it is *muri*, *mura* or *muda*? For my part, I tend to be a man with a horse who does not know how to use it.

— Rick Rowell

The kaizen model represents a customer-focused *Just in Time* process flow. The primary objective of "just in time" is the elimination of waste. Waste is understood to be anything other than the *minimum* amount of equipment, inventory, labor, space, and time that are absolutely essential to add customer value.

According to Soke, motions beyond our current capabilities (*muri*) add no value, and they are, therefore, waste. There is no need to add capacity upstream of a bottleneck; it will not add capability.

Statistical process control charts provide a conceptual framework for predicting our process capabilities and understanding the effects of unevenness (*mura*). *Mura* suggests the concept of variation; *heijo*, its opposite, describes a predictable process with very little variation and a high degree of process capability.

Taken together, *muri* (non-value-added activities) and *mura* (unevenness) can be understood to be shorthand for the time paradigm, our model for both eliminating waste (the bad costs) and adding capability (the good costs).

Muda (excess), which means you have a horse but don't know how to use it, adds yet another dimension to the time paradigm, and answers questions like this one:

> Higher frequencies mean more drops, so doesn't that mean more trucks and, therefore, more capital?

It turns out that *mura* (unevenness, a.k.a. variation) has a lot to do with *muda* (understanding how to use your horse).

The next graphic illustrates perfect *heijo* vs. typical *mura* (unevenness). When the workload varies around the clock or around the calendar, these *mura* gaps are created. You might say that on average we need only 14.3 horses, but because of *mura* we actually need 21 horses . . . nearly 50% more. So, when we focus on *muri* (non value added activities) and *mura* (unevenness), we also increase *heijo* (process capability) and we can do it with fewer horses (*muda*).

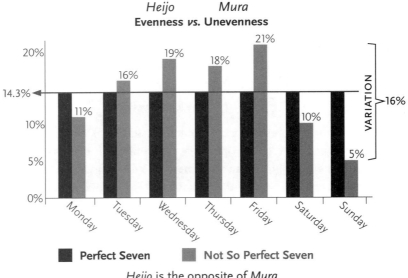

Heijo is the opposite of *Mura*

It is no wonder that what is so counterintuitive to our western culture makes perfect sense to the Japanese.

Most operations don't run seven days a week, much less 24 hours a day, but, as shown below, even with perfect *heijo*, a five day operation needs 20.5% more horses than a perfect six day operation.

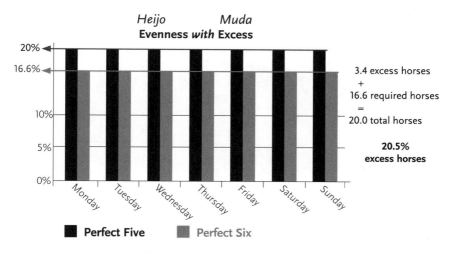

Muda means no "horse."
It does not mean that you do not have a horse,
it means that you have one and are not using it.

Seven-day operations with two shifts per day would need just over 7 horses, and that's about ⅓rd as many horses a perfect (*heijo*) five-day operation with just one shift would require.

Naturally, spreading out fewer and fewer horses (trucks) around the clock and around the calendar creates staffing opportunities (horse riders or truck drivers) for a traditional command and control organization. Nevertheless, such a large reduction of invested capital is well worth the effort, and yet another reason to shift the organization towards a process control environment.

This is especially true when you consider that the process capability to provide customer service is increased, as is the likelihood of increased thruput. Cost paradigm thinkers often miss these points, because their natural bias is the preservation of command and control and their operational focus is more towards reducing costs which remain relatively unchanged in this example.

The following graph is evidence that these *mura* and *muda* concepts are for real. Great Plains Net Asset Utilization (property, plant, and equipment) was approximately two times better than that of Coca-Cola Enterprises (CCE), the world's largest Coca-Cola Bottler, and the Pepsi Bottling Group (PBG), the world's largest Pepsi-Cola Bottler.

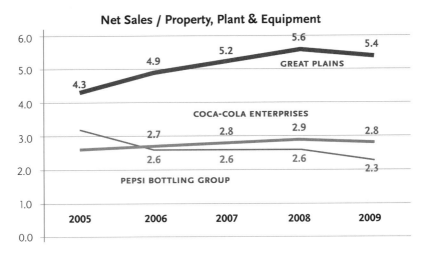

It appears that Great Plains has outperformed these companies at least since 2005. Both CCE and PBG were acquired by their parent companies after 2009, so we have no data beyond this time, but in both cases, for these years, Great Plains used far fewer horses. In fact, if both of these larger enterprises had utilized assets with Great Plains *muda* (Net Sales divided by Plant, Property, & Equipment) they could have eliminated over $5 billion worth of excess horses as shown here:

Muda in Billions	2005	2006	2007	2008	2009
Coca-Cola Enterprises	$3.1	$3.5	$3.7	$3.3	$3.1
Pepsi Bottling Group	$1.5	$1.8	$2.1	$1.8	$2.0
Total	$4.6	$5.3	$5.8	$5.1	$5.1

Over the 20 years prior to the sale of the company in 2012, Great Plains' volume increased more than 35%, from less than 18 million cases to more than 24 million cases; and the number of stock keeping units (SKUs) carried increased over 140%, from less than 200 to nearly 500. This growth was accomplished while reducing warehouse space over 40%, from over one million square feet to less than 600,000. During this same period, the fleet size shrank by more than one third, from nearly 500 trucks to less than 330; and the number of days' inventory on hand declined more than 50% from 24 to 11.

Clearly this *muda* (excess) concept is too easy . . . why doesn't everybody just do it? The answer is that it is not that easy. In order to eliminate all those horses, lots of *muri* and *mura* must also be removed. That, of course, requires time paradigm thinking, and a process control environment. For those of us caught in *the cost paradigm* this is virtually impossible.

Changing your paradigm and knowing when to do it is what the *Theory of Knowledge* is all about.

CHAPTER NINETEEN

The Theory of Knowledge

H istory has shown us that as technology advances, society lags culturally behind. In other words, we hang on too long to old theories and we are too slow to adopt new paradigms. We cling to explanations that simply describe the past, and we are too slow to develop improved theories that can better predict future outcomes. We are creatures of habit, slow to face the realization that we may have run head first into a paradox.

As the pace of change quickens, and the issues we face become more complex, the price we pay for this cultural lag can be enormous. There is a natural tendency to just apply the new technology to our problems as we have always understood them, and relentlessly pursue what used to be appropriate behavior. It is as if we are "paving over cow paths" or "recycling ignorance." Old habits really do die hard. How long we survive depends on how fast things change.

Even in a process control environment that nurtures continual improvement, there comes the time that you must know when you are in fact on a "cow path" and relentlessly pursuing what is no longer appropriate behavior. According to Deming:

> Knowledge comes from theory. You gain knowledge, only if your theory can predict a future outcome including the risk of being wrong. It is easy to describe the past. Experience teaches nothing without theory. Knowledge occurs when theory can predict future outcomes, and when this is not the case, it is time to change our theories.

Deming advocated *statistical process control*, which can determine whether a process is statistically in control, and, therefore, predictable. But as I have suggested the mathematics are daunting, and besides, it is difficult to reduce most of life's problems into mathematical expressions.

A simpler way to recognize when you have personally run into one of these paradoxes is to stay in touch with your emotions.

So again . . . think of your brain as made up of these three parts: When our thinker and our doer go out of sync, the incongruity causes our emotions to kick in and we are likely to laugh or become angry. It is a sure sign that we have either compromised our values or that we have run head first into a paradox and our theory needs to be tested.

THINKER
Perception of the Truth

FEELER
The Emotional Gap

DOER
Cultural Habits

If the incongruity affects our religion, our faith, our morality, or our ethics; then we may be tampering with what Zukav called "the seat of our soul," and Deming's advice regarding "constancy of purpose" applies. But, if it is just some economic paradox that is getting in our way, it is essential that we challenge our paradigms, and have the perseverance to change our habits.

When we are confronted with these kinds of incongruities, we naturally engage our *thinker* to level, sharpen, and assimilate the facts of our experience into a new story that makes more sense to us. This becomes our new and improved perception of the truth.

Deepak Chopra said it this way: "We must look at the lens through which we see the world, as well as the world we see, and realize that the lens itself shapes how we interpret the world."

Then gradually, with a great deal of perseverance, we develop new habits to support our new perception of the truth so that we can again delegate our behavior to the more efficient, faster reacting, and most reflexive parts of our brain, our *feeler* and our *doer*.

Gandhi complements this thinking as follows:

> *Keep your thoughts positive, because your thoughts become your words.*
>
> *Keep your words positive, because your words become your actions.*
>
> *Keep your actions positive, because your actions become your habits.*
>
> *Keep your habits positive, because your habits become your values.*

Guard your values and keep them positive,
because your values become your destiny.
This is a day, and the nurtured seed always produces
the abundant harvest.

The neuroscience supporting what I just said in layman's language is covered in great detail by Dr. Joe Dispenza in his 2012 book, *Breaking the Habit of Being Yourself*, and he summarizes this thinking in a TED Talk video linked at Sys-Tao.org. Dr. Dispenza also explains the neuroscience of why it is so hard to change our habits in another video, also found at Sys-Tao.org/links.

The question for all of us is whether this new perception of the truth is predictive of the future or just descriptive of the past.

Thought about in this way, there is no reality; everything is perception based on our assumptions (theories). Typically, and too often, especially when things *are* going our way, we tend to rationalize the past and hold on to our old theories and our old habits rather than accept what could be a better way. No wonder traditional leadership philosophies are so slow to change.

It is for these reasons that it is difficult for successful organizations to accept new technologies unless they somehow sustain their established ways. New paradigms, almost by definition, disrupt the status quo. Too often, it takes a crisis to shake the collective confidence in an obsolete paradigm. And . . . it is way harder to change an organization's cultural habits than it is to change our own personal habits.

On the other hand, it is often too risky for an individual to adopt a better theory on his own, because the politics of rejecting "what could be" for "what is" are so strong. A famous example is Galileo, who was instrumental in beginning the Scientific Revolution, but not in his own life time, because the church would not accept his teachings, and he spent the final years of his life under house arrest for heresy. It seems to be a common plight for most original thinkers, and entrepreneurs. It is as if:

The first gladiator gets the hungriest lion.

W. Edwards Deming provided us with a disruptive management paradigm in 1980, yet the question still lingers, "If Japan could, why couldn't we?" Likewise, Eliyahu Goldratt provided us with his disruptive accounting paradigm in his 1984 book. It remains a best seller, but for the most part his ideas are not yet well accepted.

Traditional leadership philosophies and accounting paradigms protect the established ways of thinking and sustain the status quo. The concepts put forth in this book under the monikers of *Thruput Accounting*, *The Time Paradigm*, and *Profound Knowledge* are by these standards disruptive paradigms that open the door to more entrepreneurial "what could be" thinking that threatens the established ways. Thought about in this way, today's management leaders are not so different than those leaders of the church over 400 years ago.

It just could be that it was easier for the Japanese to accept these "disruptive" paradigms because they already had ample "just-like" references, analogies, metaphors, and associations built into their cultural mindset. Simply said, these new ideas were already in sync with their existing perception of the truth.

To paraphrase Deming:

> Knowledge comes from theory (our thinker). We gain knowledge
> only if our theory can predict a future outcome. Experience (our
> feeler, doer) simply describes and reinforces the past. It teaches us
> nothing without theory.

An example of this has already been explained. Reconsider the paradox represented by the Company Circle vs. the Customer Circle. The first one depends on *The Cost Paradigm*, while the basis for the other is *The Time Paradigm*. They are two distinct versions of the truth based on very different assumptions (theories).

The paradox regarding how to focus on customer satisfaction and happiness while fulfilling the need for financial success of the company and its shareholders is resolved when we stand in the customer's circle. Old habits reinforce "standing in the company circle" while enlightenment regarding what could be suggests that there is a better way.

> *To become aware of what is happening I must set aside my*
> *personal prejudices or bias. Prejudiced people see only what*
> *fits those prejudices.*   **— Lao Tzu**

It takes a culture of continual improvement to nurture the acceptance of new theories, and that takes what I have referred to as "understanding relationships." A process control environment enables this type of behavior. A command and control structure shuts it down.

It takes "constancy of purpose" to establish new habits, and, in times of stress, it takes discipline not to regress to what was the old paradigm. Once again, a process control environment enables this type of behavior. A command and control structure shuts it down.

Just how challenging it is to be open to new theories and to know what is really so is illustrated by the following matrix of six *knowledge possibilities* which relate to our "thinker, feeler, and doer" (our conscious, our sub-conscious, and our habits).

KNOWLEDGE POSSIBILITIES

Know we know or — Know we don't know

Don't know we know or — Don't know we don't know

Think we know ɑ̨ we know or — Think we know ɑ̨ we don't know

My explanation of this matrix reads like this:

> *Relatively speaking, "What we know we know" is based on our conscious perception and it is tiny, but by comparison, "what we know we don't know" is microscopic because we have no perception. Likewise, "what we don't know we know" is based on our sub-conscious intuitions and it is bigger than we think, but "what we don't know we don't know" is a cosmic blind spot. Furthermore, based on our habits, "what we think we know and we know" (the right paradigm) is small, while "what we think we know and we don't know" (The wrong paradigm) is relatively large.*

> **– Bob Browne**

A simpler explanation reads like this:

> *It ain't what you don't know that hurts.*
> *It's what you know that ain't so.*

> **– Will Rogers**

	It's hard to know what is really so	
	WE KNOW	**WE DON'T KNOW**
KNOW **THINKER** *conscious*	**tiny** *perception*	**microscopic** *no perception*
DON'T KNOW **FEELER** *sub-conscious*	**bigger than we think** *intuition*	**cosmic** *blind spots*
THINK WE KNOW **DOER** *habits*	**small** *right paradigm*	**large** *wrong paradigm*

To know yet to think one does not know is best.
To pretend you know when you do not know is a disease.

– Lao Tzu

Lao Tzu seems to be telling us that we should move from the box on the lower right to the middle box . . . the one that is "bigger than we think."

In order to do this we must free ourselves from extrinsic motivations, relax, slow down, and allow ourselves to more empathically go with the flow. When we are open to all knowledge possibilities we will better know "what is really so."

The next chapter, *The Goldratt Shirt Factory* provides a good example of what happens to us when we are committed to a paradigm that does not fit the environment measured. In this case we might find ourselves in the box on the lower right thinking about GAAP Accounting, when the box to its left is a better fit. In this case the *right paradigm* is — you guessed it — Thruput Accounting.

CHAPTER TWENTY

The Goldratt Shirt Factory

What follows is a paradigm-shifting case study from the works of Eliyahu Goldratt involving a shirt factory that makes just two kinds of shirts using a simple two-step process (cutting and sewing). The problem at hand is how best to maximize cash operating profits (COP) given the *pricing*, the *product costs*, and the *market demand*.

For the time period in consideration, Total Operating Expense (TOE) is $10,000 and the capacity of the factory is 2,400 minutes on each machine for this same period of time. The market demand for each type of shirt is 120. As shown, it takes 17 minutes to make a woman's shirt and 20 minutes to make a man's shirt, so how many shirts should be made to maximize COP?

This problem is summarized in the following graphic:

The Shirt Market	WOMEN	MEN
Price	$105	$100
Product Cost	45	50
Thruput	$60	$50
DEMAND	120	120
How many shirts should we make?	?	?

Which shirt **costs** the most to make?

CAPACITY (minutes)	PROCESS TIME		
2,400	Cutting	2	10
2,400	Sewing	15	10
	Total	17	20

Cost paradigm thinking might conclude that men's shirts generate less thruput per unit, and because they take more process time, they cost more to make. A GAAP description of this situation would certainly validate this point of view. The factory should, therefore, concentrate on women's shirts.

Sewing 120 women's shirts @ 15 minutes per shirt uses 1,800 minutes of capacity, leaving 600 minutes for sewing men's shirts. Based on this, the factory should also make 60 men's shirts. Thruput for women would be 120 x $60 = $7,200, and thruput for men would be 60 x $50 = $3,000. Therefore, total thruput would be $10,200, and COP would be $200 after subtracting the TOE.

Time paradigm thinking, on the other hand, would lead to a different conclusion. Maximizing thruput per hour through the most constrained resource (sewing), would suggest that the factory should instead concentrate on men's shirts.

Sewing 120 men's shirts @ 10 minutes per shirt uses just 1,200 minutes of capacity, leaving 1,200 minutes for sewing women's shirts. Based on this, the factory should also make 80 women's shirts. Thruput for men would be 120 x $50 = $6,000, and thruput for women would be 80 x $60 = $4,800. Therefore, total thruput would be $10,800 and COP would be $800 after subtracting the TOE.

For cost paradigm believers, it is counterintuitive to think that COP could be quadrupled by focusing production on the "least profitable" product, yet common sense tells us it is so.

Goldratt would say, "Common sense that is not common practice is a paradox."

> **Economic paradox** implies a strong belief in both the measured facts, and in the theory. The resolution to economic paradoxes tends to be of the form that the data does not fit the model, or the data is not correct or, (the most common case) the model or theory does not fit the environment measured.
>
> **– Wikipedia**

As discussed before, Deming's Theory of Knowledge has to do with changing your paradigm and knowing when to do it.

> Knowledge occurs when theory can predict future outcomes, and when this is not the case, it is time to change our theories.

It appears that this might be a good time.

To further emphasize this paradox and the need to change our paradigm, consider the following Shirt Factory investment options:

Which investment to make?

	PROCESS TIME	WOMEN	MEN
The	Cutting	2	10
Current	Sewing	15	10
Situation	**Total**	17	20
Investment A = $100			
Decreases	Cutting	2	(8)
the time to make	Sewing	15	10
the least profitable shirt	**Total**	17	(18)
Investment B = $1,000			
Increases	Cutting	5	10
the time to make	Sewing	14	10
the most profitable shirt	**Total**	19	20

For cost paradigm thinkers it is counterintuitive to consider investment B that would increase the average cost per unit of the most profitable product. Instead, investing a lesser amount to decrease the average cost per unit of a less profitable product (Investment A) is intuitively a better decision. Once again, we have a strong belief in both the measured facts, and in the theory, and an economic paradox is at work on our minds.

Thruput thinkers know that thruput for the entire system is constrained by the least capable process step (sewing). When other process steps produce more than these constraints, it only builds inventory, and inventory is waste.

Decreasing process time at the constraint (sewing women's shirts) allows the system to produce five more women's shirts (1,200 of available capacity divided by a process time of 14 equals 85.7 women's shirts). Five more shirts @ $60 per shirt amounts to $300 additional thruput. The $1,000 investment (B) would pay out in three and one third production cycles. Assuming 24-hour a day operations, that's less than six days!

The $100 investment (A) increases the capacity of a resource that is not constrained, but it accomplishes nothing other than the ability to produce more waste.

Creating "economies of scale" by lowering "average costs" or increasing *capacities* upstream of a constraint does nothing to improve the capability of the total process to generate more thruput over time.

Nevertheless, cost paradigm thinkers continue to consolidate plants in order to create these "economies of scale" when all too often the real bottlenecks are far downstream from the large factories and much closer to the "Moments of Truth" at the beginning of the Demand Chain.

The Conceptual Foundations of the Sys-Tao way of leadership were explained in Part Two. Part Three of this book has been about the "what" – The principles that in so many ways disrupt our traditional leadership paradigms.

These last two chapters explained "when" we might need to change our paradigm and illustrate "why" we must be open to constantly improving our mental models.

Knowing when and why is one thing. Knowing "how" to implement these changes is more difficult. And, as already discussed, changing your mind sets off a chain reaction affecting your perception of the environment, your habits, and eventually the environment itself — these things are all interrelated. They must be thought about holistically.

The final part of this book is about *how* we were able to implement processes that embody the principles already discussed.

Systems Thinking is a good place to begin.

PART FOUR

The Process

*T*ao is a principle. Creation, on the other hand, is a process. That is all there is; principle and process, how and what.

– Lao Tzu

CHAPTER TWENTY-ONE

Systems Thinking

When you "staple yourself to an order," as in Sys-Tao, you quite literally go with the flow and find yourself on a tour of the whole process. You see all of the divergent parts (the *blue boxes*), you become aware of the rich diversity among your associates, you sense the relationships (the *green arrows*), you experience "what is," and you better understand how things happen. You develop theories about the way it could be, and that becomes your vision of the integrated whole. This is how *Systems Thinking* begins.

It is not, however, the way systems thinking developed. Most of us were introduced to the idea of systems thinking via such things as the solar system or the circulatory system of our blood flow.

Early day systems thinking was merely a mapping exercise, to better visualize big-picture ideas that were difficult to put into words. It was not until the 1950s that the idea of a negative feedback loop to control a system became popular. The idea was referred to as Cybernetics, a word whose Greek origin means to "steer" or to "navigate." These feedback loops were referred to as being "negative" because they could tell us when some measure does not meet a predetermined standard. It is like a rocket ship that is always off course just a little bit, but because of constant not-on-course feedback adjustments, the rocket always appears to be on course.

This kind of left-brained thinking got lots of us baby boomers drawing flow charts with boxes and arrows connecting other boxes, sprinkled in with triangles that represented decision points — "if yes then . . . if no then . . ." It was always so well thought out and so precise. Every effect always had a cause, or so we thought. With enough logic anything could be predetermined, or so we thought.

This approach was both mechanistic and deterministic. It kept the rocket ships on course, but those flow charts of larger and more open systems never seemed to work out the way that they were drawn. It seemed as if the world we live in was neither mechanistic nor deterministic, and that there was something very wrong with this approach. It was as if small variations between the boxes caused the system to behave in unpredictable ways — maybe you have heard about the "butterfly effect" . . . well, it can be even more unsettling than the "bullwhip effect." Furthermore, lots of those decision points were not binary — too often the answers were "maybe" or "let's talk about it." Causality seemed to get lost somewhere inside the emerging network of relationships.

It was not until about 1980 that Nobel Laureate Ilya Prigogine put his finger on the obvious exception to these mechanistic and deterministic views about systems thinking: mechanical systems are not alive, and living systems do not follow the traditional mechanistic rules of classical physics.

For instance, the laws of thermodynamics tell us that closed mechanical systems eventually run down, decay, and reach a state of equilibrium, known as maximum entropy: a measure of disorder or chaos. It is a depressing thought, but fortunately it does not apply to us humans, and it does not have to apply to the organizations we create. But to escape this fate, we must take care to create systems that can evolve in the manner of a living organism – which a command and control structure does not. It is interesting to note that in his 1984 book, *Order out of Chaos*, Prigogine wrote, "Entropy is the price of structure."

Living systems are open, self-organizing, and they are nested. They are open in that they interact with their environment and other living systems. They are self-organizing in that, as Darwin theorized, all life self-selects information and evolves itself on a genetic level over millions of years in order to "fit" in with the changing environment to survive and to thrive. Implicit with this genetic evolution is the notion that all living systems are also nested in some kind of continually evolving web of life, each species with its own survival characteristics. The process creates a continual emergence of fractal-like patterns of increasingly complex living systems.

On a daily basis the drama plays out more quickly:

> Every morning in Africa, a gazelle wakes up. It knows it must run
> faster than the fastest lion or it will be killed. Every morning a
> lion wakes up. It knows it must outrun the slowest gazelle or it
> will starve to death. It doesn't matter whether you are a lion or a
> gazelle: when the sun comes up, you'd better be running.[1]

It is as if in order to survive, living organisms actually thrive on the disorder and constant vicissitudes in their environment. In addition to those simpler negative feedback loops that we once believed to be all you needed to know, living systems possess what are often referred to as positive feedback loops that actually accelerate and amplify behavior as in this example of the lion and

---

1   Commonly attributed to Dan Montano. Originally printed in *The Economist*, 1985.

the gazelle. Furthermore, these feedback loops are not linked up in a linear way like those flow charts we used to draw. Instead, everything is networked together in a more right-brained way.

Likewise, living organisms naturally create lifelike networked organizations to further assure their survival. Birds flock, and fish school; it is difficult to find an example of a living organism that does not organize itself in some similar way. The organisms literally become nested inside their own naturally created organizations.

These lifelike organizations seem to emerge from the bottom up, in self-similar patterns that replicate based on simple rules embedded in the individual members of the population. They are in no way dictated by some leader of the pack; it is an example of emerging complexity — something very different than what the laws of thermodynamics would predict, or what some commander might attempt to control.

You can call it evolution, ecology, or sustainability, but recognize it as natural. It is the process of life. It is not *per se* doing any "thing," but it is thriving, surviving, self-regulating, and reproducing; and it has the inherent process capability to become increasingly complex as it evolves and adapts to its environment — in no way does it approach entropy.

In the case of us humans, we have evolved brains so complex that we can take this self-selected information from our environment and literally expand the neural networks of our own neo-cortex, our Thinker, with patterns of intelligence that can override our genetic instincts and our deep-seated habits. We have evolved a cerebral capability that goes beyond adaptation; we can willfully change our own environment. Unlike all others, we humans can do lots of "things" with these highly evolved process capabilities.

Over time, we developed our now-traditional top-down leadership philosophies and created command and control organizational structures that are not at all lifelike. We did it to extrinsically motivate people to get lots of stuff done. We did it despite the fact that we humans do not naturally behave in predetermined and mechanistic ways.

Paradoxically, the accelerating pace of change in our world is the direct result of these now-traditional ways of getting stuff done, but as the pace of change quickens, this continual extrinsic pressure on our feeler/doer has in some ways cut us off from our own thinkers and the ability to collaborate in a natural way. The command and control structures protect the current paradigms and resist continually evolving and newer ways of thinking. New technologies come along, but more often than not, our larger and more established organizations simply use what's new to sustain past best practices. Ironically, the ways we have structured our organizations and motivated ourselves to get things done has inhibited our ability to continually improve our paradigms, and to better cope with the change we have created.

Changing your mind is hard.
Changing your habits is harder.
Changing an organization's culture
is even more difficult.

In a process control environment, the organization is far more lifelike. It is able to thrive on the disorder and the constant vicissitudes in the environment — even if we created them ourselves. A process control environment is able to continually self-select new information from the environment and self-organize and regenerate itself in ways that are analogous to what Darwin called natural selection — but it does it in real time. It can do these things because it operates just like the human beings that are nested inside. A process control environment is simply the natural emergent complexity of even more fractal-like growth. It is as if it emerged from the neural networks of our collective "thinkers."

As these networks grow, we become increasingly capable of recognizing patterns and improving our ability to cope. We can't predict what life will bring us, but we are more capable of dealing with whatever may come our way.

Reconsider our master in the art of chess. Each player has only sixteen pieces, and the entire game is made up of just six *distinct* pieces (kings, queens, pawns, bishops, knights, and castles), each of which operates with very simple rules. Yet, as the game unfolds, there is no way to predict what fractal-like patterns will emerge as each player makes his successive move and interacts with the other player's prior move. The more games they play, the better they can recognize these patterns, and the more skilled they become, but they can not predict what will emerge from the growing complexity of the game they are playing.

The game of life is non-deterministic. We can always become better — we can always make our process more predictable — but we can never know the results. Prigogine supports this in his later book, aptly titled *The End of Certainty*.

Life is about patterns of relationships. It is these relationships that create the structure of stuff. It's not the other way 'round. In our process control model, it's more about the *green arrows* than it is about the *blue boxes*.

All systems are made up of parts — the blue boxes of the kaizen model — and in a mechanistic way, each of these parts is *dependent* on the one that comes before. For example, the accumulation of fluctuations between dependent events in a process has been shown to cause what was described as a "stack-up effect" and a common cause of excessive inventories and time delays. Theoretically, a little cybernetic engineering and a few negative feedback loops could remedy this problem, and keep the process "under control." And, if this were the case, the parts (or people) could perform independently and carry out their daily routines pretty much on autopilot.

But we now know that human organizations must be far more *inter-dependent* because small changes to one part of our system can have far-reaching effects on all the other parts. Furthermore, because we humans have evolved the ability to willfully change our own environment, these relationships must be *extremely interdependent*, just to cope with the ever-increasing pace of change that we have inflicted upon ourselves.

When networked together, these relationships create patterns of behavior and a convergence of purpose that naturally improves the process. It is just like those neurons in our cerebral cortex – when they fire together, they wire together, and create whole new ideas. Aristotle first said that the whole of a system is greater than the sum of its parts. I say that it is these interdependent green arrow relationships that make his statement true. It is only through ongoing nurturing of caring relationships between these divergent parts of the system that our organizations can become resilient to the constant vicissitudes of life and the failures of the more deterministic systems models.

These interdependent relationships require a more collaborative approach to systems thinking. It suggests an iterative cycle of first understanding "what is," then moving towards "what could be," and again re-engaging with the present, and repeating the cycle. It is similar to the "Deming Cycle" (*plan, do, study, act*). Too often, westerners interpret this cycle to be something just like the budgeting cycle, where your boss typically sets goals and later checks to see how you are doing.

But Deming was against numerical goals, inspections, and management by objectives. The Deming cycle is therefore better interpreted as a positive feedback loop in a rapidly repeating process cycle. It is about improving how the process is running rather than whether the process accomplished some goal.

This cycle describes a rhythm of periodically disengaging our faster-acting feeler/doer from "what is," and allowing ourselves to meditate and re-engage both sides of our slower-moving but more thoughtful thinker in a collaborative process of creating "what could be" and becoming better. This yin-and-yang-like cycle between "what is" and "what could be" is never just doing things; it is always self-organizing and becoming better.

Most westerners have difficulty understanding that these conceptual opposites do not belong to separated "independent functional" categories, but are extreme poles of a single "interdependent cross-functional" whole. Nothing is only yin or only yang. Everything is a relationship. All natural phenomena are manifestations of the continuous oscillation between both poles — in this case, "what is" and "what could be."

When we collaborate, we take systems thinking beyond our personal point of view. Instead, our own vision — our own version of the truth — becomes exposed to multiple points of view simultaneously, almost like a cubist painting. It is a networked point of view that seems to change based on where we are standing.

In this "interdependent" way, the green arrow relationships are creating our future and providing *purpose*. Likewise, the "dependent" functional parts, the blue boxes, provide the necessary freedom so that our diverse groups of "independent" associates will have the *autonomy* to do their own individual part. Collaboration is essential. We must always respect each other and we must always respect the process. Those are the only things we can improve, and it is the only way we can achieve *mastery*.

This is where Systems Thinking takes us. Our vision becomes shared, and it emerges into something bigger than ourselves — it becomes our calling. In this way, these three words — purpose, autonomy, and mastery — give life to our mission statement and incorporate it into a living organization.

Four videos related to the content of this chapter can be found at Sys-Tao. org/links: *Emergence — Complexity from Simplicity, Order from Chaos*; Fritjof Capra, *The Web of Life*; Michelle Holliday, *The Pattern of Living Systems, The Complexity of Life*.

In the following chapter I will explain *The Smart Order*. It is an example of something that evolved from countless iterations of this collaborative cycle of systems thinking over the past twenty years. When we sold Great Plains in 2012, The *smart order* was our current "what is." Not long before it had been "what could be." It had just evolved with us as we went around this mandala-like journey of continual improvement for all those years. As we incorporated the principles already discussed in this book, the process just got better. Each innovative improvement seemed to build on the previous one. Everything was a "just-like" reference to something that came before. Everything was inter-related. It all seemed to grow like a fractal in a recursive way — always following the same simple rules; the only thing constant was our "constancy of purpose."

The Smart Order resolves the dilemma discussed earlier — the dilemma created by the combined disruptions of *common cause variations* coming down the *supply chain* and the *bullwhip effect of special cause variations* going up the *demand chain*.

The resolution of this dilemma begins with the same three elements that are common to all systems:

- **Replenishment**
- **New Information**
- **Things Gone Wrong**

Few systems integrate them into a single seamless process:

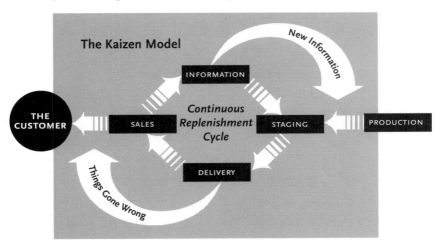

Recall the just-like reference to a "living" sewing machine used to visualize these elements in Chapter Nine. This organic sewing system includes all the attributes of the time paradigm in that it constantly creates predictably acceptable stitches at very high frequencies and with very short cycle times. You could say that this is the *replenishment* element. But what happens if we want to change the stitch, or some attribute of the thread? What is the process for telling it to do something different? This is the *new information* element.

Finally, what happens if the thread breaks? We call this element *things gone wrong*. What is the process for coping with things gone wrong?

A good process must be customer focused and capable of consistent replenishment inside the customer's specification limits. A great process can also respond quickly and predictably to new information (special cause variation), while coping with TGWs (common cause variation) in a single seamless process. A truly great process is never just doing things; it is always learning, evolving, self-organizing, and becoming better. It is the essence of creativity. It is indeed lifelike. Some might call it emerging complexity; I call it the Sys-Tao way of improving the process.

Coping with TGWs requires two distinct approaches.

Type 1 TGWs are associated with the ability to fix mistakes on the fly in real time, as characterized in the phrase:

We make mistakes, but we don't ship defects.

This approach is analogous to that rocket ship that is always off course just a little bit, but because of constant TGW corrections, it appears to always be on course. Another more lifelike analogy for type 1 TGWs is the way our body's immune system is constantly vigilant and capable of making small adjustments to ward off things that might otherwise make us sick.

Type 2 TGWs, on the other hand, can be described as:

The raw materials for improving the process

This idea is embodied in the Japanese word *kaizen*, meaning "constant incremental improvement." Kaizen stands in contrast to the western expression, "If it ain't broke don't fix it." Instead, kaizen suggests:

Everything, even if it ain't broke, can be made better.

This second approach to coping with things gone wrong, therefore, deals with the collaborative cycle of *systems thinking* as described above — continually moving "what is" to "what could be." Furthermore, it acknowledges that TGWs are either systemic and occur randomly inside the process (common cause variations), or they are the result of non-random *special causes* outside the process.

Excessive common cause variations are an indication that management needs to improve the process. In the case of special cause variations, management must either eliminate the cause or provide an additional special cause process capability to cope with it.

Whenever we go around that PDSA cycle (plan, do, study, act), we are embarking on a journey of discovering the root cause of a type 2 TGW and improving the process. One common method of doing this is to collaboratively "ask why five times" to flush out increasingly specific reasons for the problem at hand. It's a bit like the butterfly effect running in reverse. Consider Benjamin Franklin's familiar quotation:

> *For want of a nail a shoe was lost,*
> *for want of a shoe a horse was lost,*
> *for want of a horse a rider was lost,*
> *for want of a rider an army was lost,*
> *for want of an army a battle was lost,*
> *for want of a battle the war was lost...*

The smart order is a result of this kind of thinking, but as you will see, it deals directly with type 1 TGWs, keeping the rocket always on course . . . fixing mistakes on the fly in real time. It, of course, can also respond quickly and predictably to new information.

I would be remiss if I did not mention one additional type of TGW. There is a faster and more direct approach to dealing with things gone wrong. I will call it a **type 3 TGW.** This more drastic approach can be characterized by this reference from the world of sports:

Forget about the process, fire the coach, and start over.

Changes associated with these type 3 TGWs are typically sudden, exponential, and strategic (as in re-organizing, re-structuring, and re-engineering the entire company) as opposed to the more continual, incremental and tactical resolution of type 2 TGWs.

This approach can be very effective, but such vast and far-reaching changes are difficult to implement, and understanding the second and third effects of such large-scale changes is difficult to predict — because living systems are non-linear and non-deterministic. We do not naturally operate in mechanistic ways. Almost by definition, an organization's "constancy of purpose" will be disrupted by this type of change. The culture of the organization will be abruptly affected, and there is good reason to beware of the implications of these "harsh interventions."

Successful implementation of changes based on these type 3 TGWs will, therefore, sooner or later, become dependent upon a more Kaizen-like approach to Continual Improvement based on type 2 TGWs.

Ultimately, though, for any system to operate effectively at world-class levels, it must be able to cope with type 1 TGWs in real time inside a single seamless process, while responding to New Information quickly and predictably. The *smart order* is our best example. When this is the case we are no longer just doing things; we are always becoming better.

CHAPTER TWENTY-TWO

The Smart Order

An axiom:

The first step of the Demand Chain is sometimes referred to as the last mile of the Supply Chain. Value-Added Improvement begins here, at this Moment of Truth, *with the first customer in the chain, because if what we do anywhere doesn't add value here, then it is Waste.*

As explained before:

In the old days the trucks were loaded each day with a standard load from inventory produced the day before, and the route salesmen would make their daily rounds replenishing the inventory for the customers on their route.

hen opportunities regarding New Information or TGWs occurred, they were communicated directly to the route salesman who was also responsible for all aspects regarding the account. Four distinct tasks had to be coordinated:

- **Selling**
- **Ordering**
- **Delivering**
- **Merchandising**

The *selling* task entailed collaboration between the retail customer and the route salesman regarding mutual acceptance of *new information*, but, as the customers began to consolidate, this *selling of new information* task, more often than not, had to be segregated for it to occur at the customer's headquarters.

As the number of products and packages (SKUs) began to grow, a standard load no longer worked. *In-outlet ordering* was, therefore, segregated from the other tasks. Pre-salesmen were dispatched to write the orders in advance so that the right stuff could be loaded onto the trucks, but the increased Cycle Time added inventory to the total system. And, because the order was a forecast, it reduced order accuracy at the Moment of Truth.

The trend towards larger customers with more SKUs caused the industry to move to larger and more specialized vehicles, and, as a result, even the *delivery* and *merchandising* tasks were segregated from each other.

Coordinating these segregated tasks, and transmitting the agreed-to new information to the right people for the right tasks, became more challenging with each passing year.

Likewise, handling TGWs in the traditional command and control operational structures became more and more challenging. As the SKUs increased, "too much, too soon" or "too little, too late," became the all-too-common issues. They resulted in products that were either "out of date" or "out of stock."

Neither incentives nor blame could solve these problems, because the problem was not the people. It was the process, and the process was fragmenting into disparate silos separated by space and time.

Communication regarding new information and TGWs had become dependent on intermittent command and control directives. Maintaining intimate relationships between the "tasks" became more difficult, and the system was losing process capability. Likewise, because *replenishment* was now based upon a *forecast*, the pre-salesman's order became nothing more than a guess based on experience, and for the most part, our work force was young and inexperienced.

As the industry succumbed to the grip of this relentless trend toward complexity, the consolidation of bottlers continued, and it was believed that "economies of scale" would somehow solve the problem. In fact we were just adding capacity upstream of our bottlenecked distribution centers. Adding capacity upstream of these bottlenecks did not increase the system's process capability. Instead, the upstream supply chain seemed to gridlock as the increased common cause variation caused inventories to grow even more.

Likewise, the bullwhip effect further exacerbated the issue because misunderstood inventory adjustments (special cause variation caused by new information) amplified the demand signal and set off real-life beer game experiences.

And, because the newer SKUs, like Powerade, were smaller in volume and tended to come from faraway factories, truckload quantities of these small-volume items meant that their *batch sizes* were relatively larger and their *lead times* (cycle times) were longer, resulting in less frequent and less predictable deliveries of our fastest-growing SKUs. Once again, so it seemed, we always had "too much" or "too little"; inventory was either "out of date" or "out of stock."

It was as if every principle of the time paradigm was being violated. Worse yet, the time paradigm was, for most people, a cosmic blind spot.

Coincidentally, it was during this period of bottler consolidation and SKU proliferation (circa 1990) that Great Plains began the systems thinking journey towards what resulted in *The Smart Order.*

By 2006, these conditions had escalated and created a perfect storm. Great Plains was in the early stages of implementing the smart order, and The Coca-Cola Company was attempting to develop "alternative routes to market." They believed that Walmart could distribute Powerade through their own system better than the bottlers could do it. A front-page *Wall Street Journal* article featuring Great Plains chronicled the ensuing "soda rebellion" (*see* Appendix IV).

The smart order is a different paradigm. It builds on the principles of the time paradigm, it stands firmly inside "The Customer's Circle," and it operates seamlessly as a part of what has been described as a "Process Control Environment." It can replenish continuously, and it can respond in real time to both new information and TGWs in a single seamless process. It is predictable, it assures high levels of process capability, and it removes the need for "inspections." Furthermore, it requires less operating expense as well as fewer capital resources.

Looked at from a traditional supplier's perspective, and in typical industry jargon, The Coca-Cola Company had told us that it was their goal to have the "right execution daily" (RED) of their planned "look of success" (LOS) at every "point of availability" (POA) for every retail customer. This command and control jargon translates into a supplier's way of saying, "inspect what you expect." RED is an inspection program. LOS is a set of company standards (what's acceptable), and POA is generalized description of a retail inventory location for our products in a customer's store (e.g. produce aisle or front lobby).

Our retail customers, on the other hand, use different jargon to express their own unique desires. They want their store shelves to be "planogram perfect" or, in other words of the retail trade, JLP, which stands for "just like the pictures" of their planograms. Planograms, of course, is jargon for how they want each unique selling location to be set up for each stock-keeping unit (SKU). It is their way of telling us what is most desirable from the customer's point of view. Of course, it also implies that orders must be on time in full (OTIF) in order to meet these customer specifications.

Said more simply, customers want what the smart order delivers: Process capability to replenish predictably, with enough precision to assure that each unique selling location is always planogram perfect and that new information and TGWs are handled seamlessly in real time.

The smart order also improves and simplifies the demand signal that creates. It reduces the bullwhip effect, one of the primary causes of unnecessary time and inventory throughout the chain of customers we refer to as the demand chain.

Furthermore, the smart order is easy to implement, manage, and operate, because it integrates into a single seamless process the three elements that are common to all systems:

- **Replenishment**
- **New Information**
- **Things Gone Wrong (TGWs)**

Replenishment: If inventory never changed at these retail Moments of Truth, and if nothing ever went wrong — if there were no TGWs — then the customer's scanner data would be a perfect *Replenishment Order*. In other words, if whatever were scanned out of the store through the checkout registers was replenished frequently, on time, with a short cycle time, and without variation, then each "Point of Availability" (POA) could be continuously replenished on time in full, and the shelves would look just like the pictures of the customer's planograms.

Not only would the pre-salesman's guesswork go away; the pre-salesman's job could go away too. After all, this order forecasting activity is non-value-added time (NVAT) and it should be eliminated. Please note the distinction that we always valued our associates, but we did not value NVAT. It is management's job to transfer these associates to jobs where they can add value for our customers.

New information: If every time the *selling* task created a *New Information Order*, this description of what is most desirable for a specific selling location could be added to the replenishment order on the agreed-to day of execution and communicated to the Merchandiser's handheld computer with a detailed schematic of the customer's planogram. Merchandisers would know exactly how to make the inventory changes (both pluses and minuses).

Furthermore, because this new information is actually known in advance, Logistics could add temporary associates based on the upcoming workload to assure the right amount of manpower is always available throughout our kaizen model.

Likewise, supervisors would know in real time as each new information order is completed, and they would be able to fine tune the results for each unique selling location and replace the schematic planogram in the merchandiser's handheld computer with an actual picture of the desired display, including the actual inventory of every SKU in that specific location.

The entire system would know the precise inventory of each SKU authorized for each POA, and the *scanner replenishment order* would assure that every POA is always replenished on time in full just like the customer's planogram for each unique location.

In this way, because new information is separated from the replenishment order and agreed to well in advance of the planned date of execution, upstream suppliers have the best of both worlds — predictable real time *thruput information* and "known in advance" inventory changes based on the new information orders. This segregated data dramatically clarifies the upstream demand signal and the beer game is reduced to a collaborative cocktail party.

TGWs: All of this, of course, is dependent on a world without anything ever going wrong. So, whenever a merchandiser encounters a thing gone wrong (TGW) while replenishing an existing POA or while executing a change to a POA based on new information, the TGW (plus or minus) can also be reported in real time. Then the next scheduled delivery will include the *TGW Order* along with the replenishment order, and (if necessary) any new information orders.

We make mistakes, but there is no reason to ship defects when we can fix them on the fly in real time. The *smart order* process is just like that rocket ship that is always off course a little bit, but because of constant TGW corrections, it appears to be always on course.

For instance, if the inventory of a POA were unexpectedly eliminated (e.g. when a promotion is ended prematurely and a display is removed) a negative TGW order would compensate for the inventory being eliminated, and an alert (new information) would be sent automatically and in real time to the in-outlet supervisor to rectify the situation — to get the rocket back on course.

Another more subtle, even more collaborative, and more far-reaching aspect of these TGW corrections has to do with the coordination of the new information that was agreed to weeks ahead of time at the customer's headquarters. Inevitably those orders would need to be modified slightly at store level in order to satisfy the customer's unique requirements. In-outlet supervisors get this new information in their handheld computers in real time, which is ahead of time for the merchandisers. Then TGWs entered by the in-outlet supervisors automatically update the New Information throughout the system. Everyone knows what is going to happen before it happens. There is no need for inspections, because we already know what the results will be. And there is lots of time to head off future TGWs before they can occur.

In this way, intimate relationships between the segregated tasks are restored and the process itself becomes lifelike. It self-references and controls itself — just like those birds that flock.

The following graphic illustrates the methodology of how these three elements of the *Smart Order* come together to create *a perfect order*.

The *Smart Order* Methodology

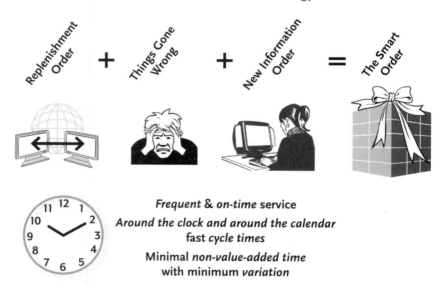

Replenishment Order + Things Gone Wrong + New Information Order = The Smart Order

Frequent & on-time service
Around the clock and around the calendar
fast *cycle times*
Minimal *non-value-added time*
with minimum *variation*

Training, productivity, and process capability are all improved for the merchandising task because there is now an actual picture in a handheld device showing what is most desirable for each unique selling location, and the ordering task is reduced to real-time reporting of TGWs. There is no guesswork or forecasts, just precise pictures of what is expected and real-time reporting of TGWs to keep the process on course.

This is not science fiction. It is working every day and everywhere Great Plains sells Cokes. It works at Super Centers and it works in barbershops.

Because the *smart order* methodology captures order entry information in these three discrete elements, the replenishment order adjusted by the TGW orders makes the customer's thruput explicit for every SKU. Likewise, the cumulative sum of the *new information* orders (pluses and minuses) tells us the actual inventory for every SKU. We are, therefore, perfectly positioned for a future in which our customers might prefer to have us consign inventory to them and then pay us based on the same scanner data their customers use to check out — this sounds like another opportunity to eliminate NVAT to me.

In the meantime, because we know the customer's thruput as well as his inventory at any moment in time, we can also know his thruput *return* on Inventory Investment (ROII) for any collection of SKUs over any period of time.

Likewise, we can know the *market pressure index* (inventory/sales) for any collection of SKUs vs. some other comparable collection of SKUs (e.g. waters vs. juices or cans vs. bottles) over any period of time. For instance, some smaller and faster-growing brands might justify more market pressure (a higher index of inventory space to sales) than some larger but slower-growing brands.

On the other hand, the portfolio of all SKUs' thruput return on inventory investment remains a worthwhile goal to be maximized. After all, thruput is our measure of *customer value*, and it keeps Wall Street happy too.

We referred to these derivative benefits of the smart order as an example of "after sales services," because they institutionalize collaborative systems thinking and make it a part of the operating process. These benefits are summarized in the next graphic.

THRUPUT   **INVENTORY**

Replenishment Order **+** Things Gone Wrong

Since we know actual
stock keeping units
in every
selling location
over any
time period
we can also know
thruput return on *inventory*
market pressure by *stock keeping unit*
(space to sales indexing)
any way we choose to mine the data.

New Information Order

In a similar way, account managers can data mine the pictures just like they can data mine the numerical data. In other words, real pictures of actual displays can be reviewed whenever and however they choose in order to draw conclusions and develop improved strategies to increase thruput consistent with their customers' expectations.

These after sales service capabilities of the smart order further assure that the process is capable of delivering the results our customers desire. They institutionalize *quality consciousness*, and *continual improvement* becomes the culture.

Most customers and suppliers lack the ability to segregate the elements of an order as illustrated in the last graphic. The next chapter, *Space, Time, and Groceries*, expands on this important fact, and explains why this particular blind spot has far-reaching implications on all demand chains.

CHAPTER TWENTY-THREE

Space, Time, and Groceries

When you are up to your waist in alligators, it is difficult to remember that it is your job to drain the swamp.

Likewise, when pricing, shelf space and days on display are the only variables, it is difficult for a supplier to distinguish the sale of groceries from inventory changes. It is easy to forget that your primary purpose is to sell groceries, or in other words, to create thruput.

Under these conditions, both customers and suppliers become compelled to focus their attention on buying and selling the shelf space and the calendars inside the stores. Terms like "slotting allowances" and "calendar marketing agreements" fill the retail lexicon as *new information* deals are negotiated to determine how many weeks certain SKUs will occupy certain amounts of the store's real estate, and at what price.

The money associated with these lucrative new information offerings obfuscates the normal thruput dollars from the sale of groceries to consumers. For instance, large displays of products are constantly in process of either being built up or taken down in order to create excitement for the retail shopper. This of course further amplifies the constant adjustments to inventory that already add noise to the demand signal going upstream. Suppliers are typically unable to distinguish these inventory changes from the groceries scanned at the checkout registers.

This is not to say that adjusting the store's space in proportion to thruput is not a good thing. It is, in fact, a very good thing. Likewise, there are times when it is wise to place more pressure (space and time) on some SKUs than others. But, without metrics to measure these activities, the system is reduced to frenetic tampering of a process that no one understands.

Looked at through the lens of *The Smart Order*, it is easy to understand what is happening. But, without the ability to separate out the new information, it is difficult to know the customer's thruput. As a result, suppliers and customers too often become engaged in what can be characterized as corporate addictive behavior. It is directly analogous to what goes on inside our brains neurologically when we receive too much extrinsic motivation, and when we depend too much on habitually driven behavior. It shuts down our *thinker*. We learn nothing from these experiences, because we have no theory — we do not have *the smart order*.

Because it is difficult to distinguish the *replenishment* needs from inventory changes (new information), the beer game erupts in full force. Every principle of the time paradigm is put to the test. Waste, unevenness, and excess (*muri, mura,* and *muda*) all increase while process capability decreases, and the likelihood of applying the wisdom of what we learned from the Goldratt Shirt Factory is lost when these chaotic circumstances come into play. Everyone reverts back to his most primitive habits.

A cliché that explains this corporate addictive behavior is:

"The best fireman is often the arsonist."

In other words: fires might occur in spite of our best efforts (TGWs that are common cause variation), but fires also occur *because* of our best efforts (special cause variation caused by camouflaged new information, a.k.a. tampering).

"High-Low" promotional pricing strategies, coupled with buying and selling space and time, clearly affects thruput, but it is difficult to know how or how much. One thing is certain: these activities create waste and destroy process capability. And, as this corporate addictive behavior escalates, market execution naturally deteriorates.

On the other hand, some customers and suppliers have come to realize that everyday low prices, coupled with logical use of space and time in proportion to normal Thruput, will yield results much more akin to a properly run Goldratt Shirt Factory. Furthermore, *waste* is reduced and market execution is improved. The beer game settles down, asset utilization improves, and the business tends to outperform the competition.

Life is good for some.
How long the others survive
depends on how fast things change.

The next chapter is designed for left-brained thinkers who need even more tangible explanations of *The Smart Order*.

CHAPTER TWENTY-FOUR

Predictive Replenishment

By definition, scanner data measures the volume associated with thruput. Theoretically, it is the right metric, but operationally it is not practical for *direct store delivery* suppliers because there is no standardization of operating criteria among retail customers for obtaining this information in a reliable and timely way.

So how can we predict what the scanners will tell us?

The answer is a fairly straightforward math problem. The average of the past seven deliveries for a given day (e.g. Monday) net of any new information orders during that time period is a very good prediction of the scanner data for Mondays.

The reason for netting out new information is that, by definition, it is a "change in inventory," and it is not thruput.

The reason for averaging just Mondays in this example is to compensate for common cause variations within the week.

The reason for averaging "seven" deliveries is somewhat arbitrary. It is large enough to be statistically significant and small enough to not pick up significant seasonal trends.

So, if on the past seven Mondays 800 cases were delivered, but 100 were new information orders, then the deliveries net of new information would be 700, and the scanner prediction (700 divided by 7) would be 100.

Once this is determined, an easy way to maintain this *predictive replenishment* number is to simply adjust the prediction by the amount of the previous TGW order.

For instance, if a TGW order of 14 had been placed on Sunday, the next delivery's *Total Order* (Monday in this example) would be increased by 14, making it 114, and the following Monday's Replenishment Order would be 714 divided by seven, which equals 102.

The point here is that we do not really need scanner data to get a good replenishment order, because it is operationally easy to predict, and the previous TGW order (e.g. Sunday's adjustments) keeps "the rocket always on course."

In other words, scanner data does nothing to compensate for the stack-up effects of common cause variations coming down the supply chain (see Chapter Sixteen — *Second Semester Variation*). TGW adjustments compensate for this automatically, as well as adjusting the replenishment process for changes in demand.

Accuracy depends on *the time paradigm*. It is important that cycle times and frequencies not vary and that deliveries are on time. What customer would not want that? Likewise, faster and more often is always better because it reduces the common cause variations that are inherent in any process. Reducing variation makes the process more precise and more capable of providing *quality* for the customer.

This is also a big step towards product supply planning, because we can pretty much know the predictive replenishment order "all the time."

The new information orders (inventory changes), on the other hand, are special cause variations, because they are non-random and extraneous to the process. Importantly, though, we can know these new information orders well in advance of their scheduled deliveries.

This allows us to take what was explained in Chapter Fifteen (*Understanding Variation*) to another level. We already know that increasing the frequency and thereby reducing the drop sizes will reduce variation of the total orders. This was shown before and the illustration is repeated here.

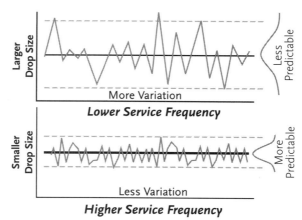

It follows that separating the *new information orders* (special cause variation) from the *total order* and focusing only on the *replenishment orders* will further reduce the *variation*.

The next two graphics illustrate this variation-reducing effect of unbundling the new information orders from the total orders.

When we unbundle the new information (the bars in the second graph) from the total order (the solid line in the first graph) and apply the remaining principles of the time paradigm, it drives the replenishment process (the dashed line) closer to perfect *heijo* (a system without variation). The predictive replenishment order becomes even more precise, and the *muda* (excess horses or trucks in this example) begins to melt away.

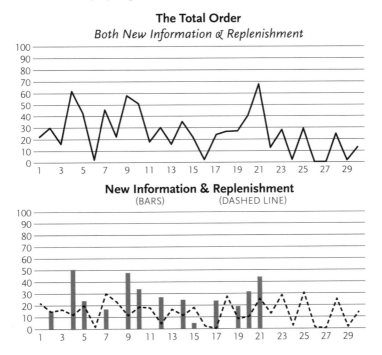

The Total Order
Both New Information & Replenishment

New Information & Replenishment
(BARS)   (DASHED LINE)

This very predictable and always-known base line information simplifies scheduling of all kaizen model activities. For instance, fixed delivery frequencies affected only by common cause variations assure that consistent service levels are matched to customer needs. Likewise, merchandising schedules can then be handled in a similar way.

Production scheduling and staffing of warehouse operations can also be matched to these predictable replenishment orders. This same information is valuable to upstream suppliers who can operate off of standing orders for thruput replenishment.

Naturally, we are left to think about the new information (special cause variations) separately, but that is a good thing, because we know the new information "ahead of time."

This opens the door for management to develop *special cause process capabilities* to take care of the new information (inventory) surges and keep the replenishment process running smoothly and on time and on schedule.

Customers want frequent, consistent, and on-time service; so it is important that *delivery* and *merchandising* run on time and on schedule, just like bus routes that are affected only by common cause variations.

There are, however, times when special cause variations, caused by new information orders, are so big that the buses run out of *capability*. Jokingly, the Bus Route motto might be, "You call, we haul, no job too small, some too big."

But, because new information orders are known in advance, *logistics* can supplement these fixed bus routes with support from what might be called *special cause routes*. We called them *911 Routes* because they are *not* fixed like the bus routes. 911 routes, just like the name implies, are dynamic and can go whenever and wherever excessive new information orders call for it.

So, when orders exceed the normal process capability, the system is able to call 911 without disrupting the bus routes. The *total orders* are simply the sum of what we pretty much know "all the time" plus what we know "ahead of time." So, why forecast it, if you already know the answer? If necessary, just call 911 ahead of time.

Forecasting
There is no reason to do well,
what should never be done at all.

Too little
Capability   Too much
                                              Waste

OUT OF STOCK   Just in Time   OUT OF DATE
        TOO LITTLE   TOO MUCH

Thought about in this way, our traditional approaches to planning give way to more nimble methods of institutionalized collaboration and coordination. The command and control structure fades away and a self-organizing system without departmental boundaries emerges. As the needs for forecasting begin to disappear, you can almost visualize inventories self-regulating like those birds, always maximizing *thruput*, always minimizing stack-up effects, and always executing the desired "look of success" at each and every unique selling location. It is a form of emergent complexity that comes up from the bottom — there is no head bird (*see* Dylan Winter and the *Starling Murmurations* at Sys-Tao.org/links).

CHAPTER TWENTY-FIVE

How We Did It

J ust *how* we implemented the processes, which embody the principles discussed in Part Three of this book, has already been suggested. For instance, the *Smart Order* was not planned; it evolved. It emerged slowly along the way of what could be described as a fractal-like journey of *continual improvement*.

Fractals are a pretty trendy and seemingly hard-to-understand mathematical concept that has been used often in this book. Suffice it to say that fractals are self-similar patterns that replicate based on a simple set of rules. Thought about in this way, it becomes easier to visualize how complex systems can emerge naturally from simple patterns of relationships. To witness examples of fractal growth, and to better understand the significance of this important concept, see *The Hidden Dimension* at Sys-Tao.org/links.

Metaphorically, the rules for our fractal-like journey are analogous to the five customer service process platforms that developed in a very pragmatic way and later evolved as the basic architectural backbone of our Management Information Systems. Everything we did seemed to self-reference in accordance to these five process platforms:

· **The Replenishment Process**

· **The New Information Process**

· **The TGW Process**

· **The Special Cause Process (911)**

· **The After Sales Service Process**

The first three of these are prominently embedded in the smart order and in our kaizen model of a process control environment. The fourth followed closely behind, but the last platform — *After Sales Service* — came relatively late in the order of things. Looking back, it strikes me that it took all five of these platforms to make up the "DNA" of what emerged at Great Plains. These five process platforms served us well, and for us there was no sixth platform. This is it — it really is that simple.

Continual Improvement became easier once we developed this fractal-like blueprint on which to build our systems. Like all things fractal in nature, what eventually emerged seemed incredibly complex when in fact it was so very simple. These process platforms can apply to any organization, and the same holds true for the principles discussed earlier. But that brings me to yet another paradox.

These principles did not come to us first. The principles were, of course, always there, but we did not become fully aware of them until we had evolved all five of these process platforms. And they did not just appear one Sunday afternoon. So, how did we do it?

To explain this will require another brief digression. When we learn new things, we naturally seek concept before detail. Consider the following:

> With hocked gems financing him, our hero bravely defied all scornful laughter that tried to prevent his scheme. "Your eyes deceive," he had said. "An egg, not a table, correctly typifies this unexplored planet." Now three sturdy sisters sought proof. Forging along, sometimes through calm vastness, yet more often very turbulent peaks and valleys, days became weeks as many doubters spread fearful rumors about the edge. At last from nowhere welcome winged creatures appeared, signifying momentous success.

Without first understanding the overall concept of the passage it is unlikely that you would comprehend much; and it is also likely that you would remember very few details. But, when told it is about Christopher Columbus, you probably understand very well and remember a lot. Knowing his name unlocks the door to your "meaning network."

Understanding concept before detail is not unlike understanding principle before process. In the case of this book, I have explained the Sys-Tao philosophy by sharing the principles first, before explaining the processes that evolved.

As we make our way through life, new experiences cannot exist in thin air. We naturally seek familiar concepts that we can attach these experiences to. What this means is that all new learning is somehow dependent upon internal self-referral to existing neural networks, to past paradigms, to what we already think we know and hold meaningful — to the principles we already understand.

On the other hand, the philosophy I have described as "Sys-Tao" is based on a very different conceptual foundation — one that has no meaning network for most of us. Without a prior concept of Sys-Tao and the principles that underpin it, how could we make this transformation? Changing deep-seated concepts and well-established habits does not happen by just reading a book. It brings us full circle back to this trilogy:

Changing your mind is hard.
Changing your habits is harder.
Changing an organization's culture
is even more difficult.

We could not explain new paradigms or new leadership principles to our people — we did not fully understand them yet ourselves. We did not send anyone to "collaboration school" or try to change people's habits. Management did, of course, adopt and embrace these paradigms and principles, but not as a result of some sort of training — it happened more by way of discovery — it was part of the journey, and it took time.

The journey began innocently, but almost ended suddenly with a crisis of my own making when we were introduced to the Teamsters union.

Looking back, I now realize that our early more mechanistic approach to "systems thinking" had fragmented our associates into three groups: A senior management group (myself and a few others that I will refer to as "we"), our managers and supervisors, and our front-line associates — the ones who get the work done at the moment of truth facing a customer, whether internal or external.

The inflection point of our transformation began with our (senior management's) shift of focus towards what has been described as *quality consciousness* — the understanding of what our customers considered to be most desirable. We began to realize that our own associates were our most important customers. Slowly and without realizing it, we had begun shifting our focus from the "company circle" towards the "customer circle" — we had "stapled ourselves to an order," and we were becoming increasingly aware that the process was more for our customers than it was for us.

As we focused more on these aims and less on our goals, more on what is desirable for our customers and less on what is acceptable for us, the culture began to shift to a more natural way of being. Our first-line — moment of truth – associates liked this new approach from the very beginning.

When fear, blame, carrots, and sticks begin to leave the workplace, it becomes easier to mentally shift from "doing things extrinsically," to "thinking about processes intrinsically" and then to refocus back again to "getting things done." Importantly, this cycle of activity between "what is" and "what could be" *feels* better too. Evaluating the process and not blaming the people did not happen quickly, but it did happen. "Constancy of purpose" was critical, because it was difficult for our managers and supervisors to just stop playing the "blame game."

For the most part, our managers and supervisors understood what we were aiming for, but they did not yet know how to manage a process for improvement (and neither did we). It was difficult for them to stop holding people accountable for results. And now, we were holding them accountable for the process too.

Occasional "harsh interventions" would set us back. "Constancy of purpose" would pick us up. Despite these "old habits" and the lack of newer and better ways to measure the process, the momentum increased as we began to create more and more processes built upon these first four customer service platforms.

As explained, our front-line associates welcomed this emerging corporate culture, but our managers and supervisors increasingly felt like they could no longer manage their own organizations. It was not long before this rip tide of conflicting cultures opened the door for the Teamsters. Based on our encounter with the union, there was good reason to question whether we could sustain these emerging patterns of improvement. We were literally changing our minds, but our old habits were still holding us back.

We lacked a concept to attach the details to, and we had no idea how to "manage a process," but *continual improvement* did become easier once we developed this fractal-like blueprint on which to build our systems. We of course had to remain customer focused, and we had to believe that good things would always emerge when we improved our processes in this way. It is a bit ironic that we never fully appreciated the underlying principles or understood how to "manage a process" until we were well along the way of simply improving processes for our customers.

Yet, all of life seems to have evolved from self-similar patterns based on seldom-understood common principles. The diversity of what continues to evolve is infinite — this is what I mean by "emerging complexity." We really did not know where it was taking us, but it seemed to be a better place. The same holds true for the organizations of all things living — we are nested by nature, and our organizations are extensions of ourselves. To function for us, I realized that our organizations must be alive like us.

Ultimately it is the organization's culture that must change, and if the organizational environment does not enable a culture of continual process improvement, changing your mind without being able to change your habits will only make you miserable.

Based on my experience with Coca-Cola, the secret formula to a successful transformation is the creation of a process control environment. A process control environment enables this kind of cultural change — it is profoundly different than managing people for results. Continual process improvement is not sustainable unless the culture changes too — that is what enables managers to change their habits.

There was no recipe. It was a journey, and it can only be explained as a story. I am sure it will be the same for anyone else who chooses to transform their own traditional ways to something more along these lines. Everyone's story will emerge in slightly different ways – the destination is not certain, but the Sys-Tao way is clear.

So let's flash all the way back and see how this journey began. Regarding leadership philosophies, my personal background could not have been more traditional, and yet along the way my philosophies were completely transformed. Anecdotally, I will explain some of the transformational trigger points and give examples of how these five process platforms evolved and became the DNA for this journey.

The important takeaway is not the steps we took. It is the steadfast faith that if we remained customer-focused and dedicated to always improving our process capabilities, it would take us to a better place. We had very few goals, but our aim was always to become better — and we did.

PARALLEL LEARNING

Professor John Seddon talks about the seminal moments that led to the evolution of his systems thinking method in this 2009 video (Sys-Tao.org/links) His 2005 book, *Freedom from Command and Control*, in many ways, parallels the thinking in this book.

CHAPTER TWENTY-SIX

Great Plains and Me

I was born January 7, 1943 on the front wave of the Baby Boomer Generation and with a silver spoon to boot. After all, I was in line to be a third-generation Coca-Cola Bottler.

I grew up in Oklahoma City, worked summers at the Coke Plant, did well in school and ended up at Williams College, a small liberal arts college in western Massachusetts.

I graduated from Williams in 1965 with a degree in Art History and decided to join the Navy. I received my commission from Officer Candidate School in 1966, then served aboard ship in Vietnam and on shore in San Diego until 1969. I liked Williams better, but I am as proud of my military service as I am of my college degree.

After the Navy, I attended Columbia University in New York City where I got my MBA in 1970. That same year I met my wife Karen. We were married in 1971, and I am way more proud of that than any other of my accomplishments.

As Deming might say, she is my constant source of joy, and I am her Continual Improvement project.

After two years of work experience in New York City with Arthur Andersen & Company (one of the largest public accounting firms at the time), Karen agreed that I still had Coke in my veins, so we moved back to Oklahoma City in 1973 to join the family business.

There were still over 550 bottlers of Coca-Cola in the United States in 1973. By then, my granddad was 95 years old and my dad was 67. Clearly, it was a good time for me to return to my cultural roots and start another generation for this well-established and very traditional business.

Our daughter, Cori, was born in 1973; and our son, Web, was born in 1978. Today, they are both married with families of their own.

Seven years after Karen and I moved back to Oklahoma, my granddad Virgil died. Upon his death, I realized that not a single shareholder of our company had ever bought or sold a single share of stock, and every one of them had inherited their shares from one of the original founders. No single shareholder owned even 10% of the total shares, and there were already over 65 shareholders with many more waiting in the wings for their inheritance.

I had even figured out that each of my kids might someday own about 1% — if my dad, and then I, saw fit to be so charitable. It of course did not occur to me that my grandchildren would be reduced to less than one half of 1%.

But as it turned out that was not an option, because this diverse group of shareholders was beginning to grow restless. They lacked liquidity; we had made some acquisitions, put on some significant debt, and, as a result, reduced their dividends. The industry continued to consolidate, and it soon became clear that our shareholders were ready to sell out too.

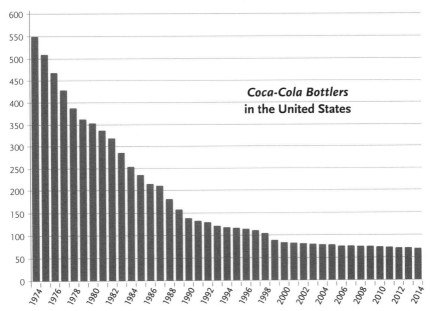

Those first seven years back in Oklahoma might someday be the subject for another book, but for now, suffice it to say that on April Fool's Day, 1980, my brother Henry and I, with the financial help of two investors, Frank M. Late and Robert S. Bowers, bought the business. We paid nearly $45,000,000. Henry and I represented 25% of the deal – mostly in sweat equity, because most of the real money came from our investors.

At the time I had never heard the term "LBO" (leveraged buy-out), but afterwards I realized that is what we had done. The company was heavily leveraged (our debt-to-equity ratio was more than 6X, and interest rates were over 20%), but we owned it, and I was Chairman and CEO. There were still 350 Coca-Cola Bottlers in the United States, and I was just proud to be one of them.

Nothing in my background, management training, or experience had anything to do with the principles set forth in this book.

> The Navy had given me invaluable experience, but it was in a highly functionalized command and control organizational structure.
>
> At Columbia, the MBA program emphasized the importance of creating shareholder wealth via approaches like what I described earlier as solving Type 3 TGWs.
>
> The so-called Total Quality Management (TQM) movement had not yet begun, and nothing offered at Columbia related to any of Deming's teachings. Likewise, Goldratt's book, *The Goal*, was not published until 1984. (It is, however, interesting to note that Deming later taught at Columbia from 1985 until his death in 1993.)
>
> At Arthur Andersen, I worked in the firm's management consulting division — which today is called "Accenture." Their consulting practice was a strong proponent of something they called "Responsibility Reporting," which was their way of selling MBO (Management by Objectives) systems to their clients.

After taking charge of Great Plains in 1980, we accelerated these "old paradigm" ways for at least seven more years.

I like to call these the Upton years, because our COO (Chief Operating Officer) at the time was an ex-Marine named Bob Upton. We had both been in Vietnam. He used to say, "The Marine Corp builds men." I would retort, "If you're not a man the Navy doesn't want you." We were quite a pair.

Everything we did was focused on exploiting economies of scale so that we could take market share away from the competition, pay down debt, and increase shareholder wealth. There was very little regard for solving customer problems, and we were very much self-centered and in the "company circle." For us, every opportunity was a type 3 TGW.

We instituted elaborate MBO systems and complex incentive pay plans for everyone. Competition among peers was encouraged. Whether you got results mattered. How you got results was more like a trade secret for experienced workers than a well-understood operating process. Without apology, we encouraged and rewarded islands of excellence inside of our highly functionalized and manipulative command and control hierarchy, and we were proud of it.

We had no idea that these islands of excellence could also be creators of waste, and it was nearly ten years before I began to realize the meaning of the cliché, "the best fireman can be the arsonist." In other words, most of our "fires" were happening *because* of our best efforts, not *in spite* of them. Pogo was right: "we had met the enemy and he was us."

An example that comes to mind has to do with our Enid, Oklahoma, distribution center (DC). At the time, DC managers were rewarded each month according to incentives based on increases in volume, gross profit, and operating profit.

Our DC managers, in turn, became skilled at manipulating our incentive pay system. When faced with what appeared to be insurmountable hurdles, like outperforming a particularly good month from the prior year, they would heavy up on discretionary expenses, such as topping off their fuel storage tanks, and hold back on activities that would drive volume and gross profit. Then, when cycling a bad month, they would do the opposite.

The punch line to this story is that once upon a time, when we were cycling a particularly bad month, there was a day when some of our trucks were unable to run because they were literally "out of gas!" That's right; our DC manager had refused to buy diesel fuel that month because he was trying to make his bonus.

Little did we realize that our elaborate schemes to incentivize performance were, in fact, resulting in tampering (introducing *special cause variation* into a system that was already overburdened with excessive *common cause variation*), and we were actually causing more fires than we were putting out.

This realization, for me, began during a three-year period in the late 1980s when we were able to nearly double our size through a series of acquisitions. Conventional (Type 3) wisdom had led us to believe that we should shut down the newly acquired production facility and consolidate its output into our Oklahoma City facility in order to exploit the "obvious" economies of scale.

In order to implement this plan, we gradually shifted production to our Oklahoma City operation, and for over a year's time we wound down the newly acquired plant.

Each of our highly incentivized DC managers placed beer-game-like pressures on the Oklahoma City facility as they built inventories of safety stock to protect their own self-interests. The Oklahoma City plant manager naturally felt the need to increase batch sizes in order to cope with the increased demands, and this only exacerbated the issues because the DC managers then felt the need to further increase safety stocks. As we continued to shift production to the Oklahoma City plant, things just got worse.

At the time, we did not have words for what we were experiencing, but in hindsight I now know that we had violated every principle of the Time Paradigm. And not only had we created yet another episode of the beer game, but we had also become another case study of what happens when you miss the point of Goldratt's Shirt Factory.

The ultimate irony of these chaotic times is that, as we wound down and simplified the operations of the plant we were about to close, we actually received the National Presidents Award from The Coca-Cola Company for the quality performance of the plant we were closing!

Naturally, the key business indicators had improved for that plant, because we had shifted so much complexity to the Oklahoma City plant. To this day, this is my favorite example of the expression, "islands of excellence and creators of waste." And, just think, we were about to shut down our island of excellence.

It was as if we were "creating bottlenecks" faster than we were filling bottles.

By sheer coincidence, it was during this time that I read *The Goal*, became familiar with the Total Quality Management movement, learned about Deming, and met John Ustas.

John Ustas was a very frustrated young plant manager who was running the Pepsi-Cola operation in Oklahoma City. He was frustrated because his bosses wanted him to close the Oklahoma City Pepsi plant and consolidate the operations into their Tulsa, Oklahoma plant. The Pepsi strategy was virtually identical to ours, and John was dead set against it.

John's frustration caused him to call me in order to pursue career opportunities within the Coke system. I told him about our strategy, and he convinced me that I was wrong. We had both been reading the same books, but John realized sooner than I that consolidating capacity upstream of our bottlenecks would not increase thruput over time; it would only increase inventories and cycle time. I like to describe the next seven years as the Ustas years.

John joined Great Plains in 1989 as Vice President of Manufacturing, reporting to Bob Upton. They did not get along. John was very much a systems thinker — albeit a *mechanistic* systems thinker — and Bob Upton was very much a Marine.

My paradigm was already shifting, and Bob Upton resisted the direction John and I were headed. As a result, Bob left Great Plains in 1990 to run the Coca-Cola operation in Boston.

The Ustas influence was all about the Sys in Sys-Tao. John had little regard for the Tao. Said another way, he, at that time, lacked what Deming referred to as Understanding Psychology, and neither of us yet understood *collaborative* systems thinking.

John's mechanistic approach to systems thinking was invaluable, but his lack of sensitivity to the Tao proved to be a problem. As John implemented change, his "harsh interventions" with our work force began to take a toll on his effectiveness with the people. In 1993 the Teamsters Union unsuccessfully attempted to organize our work force. We pressed on and implemented the first generation of what was to become four of our five process platforms:

- **The Replenishment Process**
- **The New Information Process**
- **The TGW Process**
- **The Special Cause Process (911)**

We all grew and became better during the Ustas years, but in 1998, when the Teamsters Union again attempted to exploit the resulting unrest, it became necessary for John to move on too.

The Teamsters were again unsuccessful, and since leaving Great Plains, John has had the opportunity to run Coke's operations in Norway and India, and today he is the managing director for Coca-Cola's operations in South Africa. We remain friends, and I hold him in the highest regard.

We all learn from our past TGWs. With Bob Upton I learned that "the best fireman is often the arsonist." Bob Upton and I did it the traditional way, we were successful in that we got results, and we created a lot of excitement, but we also set a lot of fires along the way and did very little to improve the process. With John Ustas we were again successful, but I learned that "harsh interventions" destroy caring relationships, and without caring relationships precise systems cannot be sustained. We improved the process, but we were unable to improve the culture.

We all learned from our time together. All of us were younger then, and hopefully, we are wiser now.

CHAPTER TWENTY-SEVEN

The Emergence of Five Platforms

Most of the process improvements during the Ustas years were the precursors to what we later referred to as *Single Source Supply.*

Simply stated, this idea means that each customer should be satisfied by just one supplier. We at first focused on what became known as our *Replenishment Platform.* On a larger scale the intent was to streamline what is most often referred to as the logistics of sending goods and services down the supply chain "just in time."

For instance, we had learned from our attempted plant closing that being close to the market, with quick response to changes, was far better than forecasting our needs upstream to multiple facilities. So we reversed our previous decision and kept both plants operating, but it was impractical to produce every SKU at both plants. Then we devised a shuttle system, so that what was not produced in one plant could be shuttled to the other and vice versa. In that way, each production facility could be the "single source supplier" for its customers – our distribution centers (DCs).

And, on a smaller scale, we also began to trace the flow of an order going up what we began to call the "demand chain." We began asking ourselves questions like: Why can't the person who answers the phone answer the question too? Why do we transfer so many calls? This type of questioning seemed to apply to everything we were doing. In our attempts to be a single source supplier, we were, without realizing it, beginning to focus on eliminating non-value-added time and reducing cycle time.

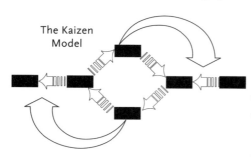

The Kaizen Model

As we drew those early day flow charts, we kept coming up with the same blinding flash of the obvious: No matter how we scaled our drawings, whether our diagrams were about the big picture or the tiniest details, they always had the same fractal-like structure. We always had stuff flowing to the left and information flowing to the right. In concept it was all so simple, but in reality, it was separated by too many organizational silos, and it took way to many steps (blue boxes) to draw a meaningful picture of what was . . . well, not happening.

The DNA of our flow charts looked like our kaizen model, but our organization looked more like *blue boxes* stacked up in the shape of a pyramid. The information went up and down and the stuff went sideways across the bottom. Looking back, our "what is" was hard to draw, and our "what could be" was easy to draw, but difficult to imagine.

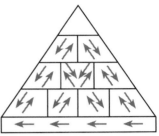

Nevertheless, we postulated that if we could just replenish each distribution center (DC) with what they sold each day, a standard pre-set inventory would give each DC all the safety stock they would ever need. It was just another example of our early mechanistic approaches to systems thinking.

It worked, but it was not easy to implement, because only John and I had accepted this new paradigm, and we just forced it on the organization.

The next logical step was to reduce each DC's inventory to zero, and send loads prebuilt for each delivery truck's route so that the shipment could be cross-docked (moved directly from the transport vehicle to the delivery vehicle) at each distribution center for same-day delivery. It became our vision, our next "what could be."

We were getting pretty good at the *replenishment process*, and we were developing some pretty good negative feedback loops for control purposes. But, "negative" here also took on a new meaning, because our DC managers did not appreciate what we were doing. In their eyes we were removing important degrees of management discretion. Without realizing it, we were beginning to dismantle their command and control authority over their own operation, and they did not like it.

These precise systems required far more coordination, and our well-established management by objectives and incentive systems were forcing our managers deeper into their own silos in order to protect what management discretion they still had. We felt as if they were tampering with our well-thought-out plans. On the other hand, they felt as if they were losing control of something that only they fully understood.

We reasoned that it was our management by objectives system that was causing them to tamper with these processes, so we eliminated the incentive systems. We told them to "manage *for* objectives" instead of "managing *by* objectives." In other words, we told them to "manage the process," but they had no tools for managing the process — they didn't even like the process — and we had taken away their main tool for managing the people.

And they still had to coordinate selling, ordering, delivering, and merchandising; but now they had to do it without inventory, with less discretion over their own work force, and they were to do it without carrots, just sticks! It has been said, "If the only tool you have is a hammer, every problem looks like a nail." We needed ways to measure the process, and we needed to quit blaming (hammering) the people.

That was also about the time (circa 1995) that we first introduced the idea of a process for "things gone wrong." There was plenty going wrong, and we didn't want to hear it all from our disgruntled managers. Associates were told to "call in" their TGWs to our newly formed "Customer Information Center," rather than waste time trying to track down their supervisor. TGW feedback from our first-line associates at the *moment of truth* was well accepted. It is a simple way to report any work-related issues — "Anytime anything goes wrong, just call the customer information center." They didn't have to worry about telling their boss, "Just report the TGW and go on with your job." Our distribution center managers, on the other hand, viewed this as yet another way to circumvent their authority.

Shortly after that we began experimenting with the idea of sending out what we called "executables" (new information) using our then-state-of-the-art "pagers." These "executables" were not a high-tech way for our straw bosses to dispatch directives. Instead, they were a way for us "big bosses" to dispatch "new information" for marketing purposes. We had correctly determined that distractive command and control directives from supervisors tended to pull workers from their bus-route-like assigned tasks, so we decided to use this "new information" capability to tell the process when and how to do something different, and it would be dispatched from logistics (which was also a part of the Customer Information Center). Needless to say, this further exacerbated the frustration of our managers and supervisors. It seemed as if we had eliminated yet another degree of management discretion from their quiver of capabilities.

To make matters worse, in the eyes of these managers and supervisors, we initiated a fourth, "special cause," platform. As explained earlier, we called it "911." It was for situations that were beyond our system's normal capabilities — situations that would take our "bus routes" off course. For instance, if a customer's planogram was changed in a significant way, and there was not enough time or resources for the assigned merchandisers, we could "call 911."

They initially perceived 911 as a motor pool of workers to be tapped in times of emergency, and they welcomed the idea. But we again disappointed them when it became clear that these 911 people would be routed ahead of time by logistics as deemed necessary, in order to supplement planned-for excessive "new information" requirements. Once again, they felt as if we had taken away their ability to manage their own people in their own organization.

We were trying to automate the flow of information within our kaizen model in order to complement the flow of goods and services, but too often it was not going our well-planned way. Our mechanistic approach to developing deterministic models, that seemed to work perfectly on paper, too often failed to work in the real world — and we did not know why.

For instance, our next idea of working "around the clock and around the calendar" (24/7/365) again made sense on paper, so we pressed on. More success was followed by more paradigm-shifting resistance. The need for more precision was closely followed by the need for more cooperation and less tampering. John and I were demanding and commanding more, but we were also dismantling the preexisting relationships and we had not replaced them with anything of equal or greater value. We had changed our minds — our paradigm — and we had just expected our managers and supervisors to change their habits. We had created process control, but it was being controlled by "us" — a singular corporate brain — and in the eyes of our managers and supervisors it was not working because life doesn't work that way. Life is far more relational and far less deterministic than our mechanistic models suggested, and we would need much more than technology to make our ideas work.

Nevertheless, as we experimented with better methods for sending and receiving TGWs and new information, and as we refined our replenishment capabilities with the addition of a special cause process, we gained confidence in the merits of these four simple platforms that seemed to apply to everything we were doing:

- **The Replenishment Process**
- **The New Information Process**
- **The TGW Process**
- **The Special Cause Process (911)**

They made such perfect sense from our linear point of view — If only our people would execute our plans, we could automate any process with these four basic building blocks. Nevertheless, there was something terribly wrong. As we continued to improve the process our managers and supervisors continued to hold their people accountable for results. For that matter, we were holding our managers accountable for implementing our new processes.

We would tell our people to just follow the process, but whenever the process failed, we were all too often blaming them for the results. It was as if we were shooting the messenger when we received TGWs. Our moment of truth associates liked our new systems, but they did not like the retributions that came with just following the process. We had not changed our old habits and our culture was in disarray.

By 1998 our people were again beginning to like the Teamsters more than our new ways of getting stuff done. It became clear that we needed something more than our mechanistic approach to systems thinking.

We needed a more collaborative approach. In fact, we needed real-time collaboration around the clock and around the calendar for whoever was on duty, irrespective of what bosses were in charge of the functional silos. Bosses don't work all the time, and neither do any of our associates. The process never stops, and it can't depend on bosses for approvals any more than bosses can assume that any particular individual will always be on duty. The "Voice of the Process" needed to be more like those birds that flock than some boss who rules.

Metaphorically, we needed to be more like all other living organisms — nested inside a "living" organization — so that our entire organization could operate more holistically. After all, everything was moving way too fast for any one bird to command and control a flock like all of us.

If one bird could no longer direct the group, this implied that the entire flock must have a common aim and "constancy of purpose." Only then could this ongoing collaboration always assure *continual improvement*. It would become management's primary job to nurture this collaborative process — something profoundly different than managing people for results.

A young manager in our company by the name of Comanche Thomas was instrumental in the development, and more importantly, the implementation of our early stage *collaborative systems thinking* improvements. And, yes, Comanche is an American Indian, and, yes, understanding relationships came naturally to him. He understood both the Sys and the Tao. In fact, it was during the unrest that preceded the Teamster's first unionization attempt that we began our Sys-Tao (Staple Yourself to an Order) process tours and made that first Sys-Tao movie. It emphasized in a holistic way the caring relationships that linked all of our emerging processes, and it became an integral part of our training for the next twelve years.

John left because of the Teamsters in 1998, and we were again able to defeat the union and persuade our associates that our emerging Sys-Tao philosophy was the better choice. Comanche was later forced to leave due to unfortunate medical circumstances in 2005. Without Comanche, I am confident that our efforts would have stalled. Likewise, without John Ustas, we may well have never started the journey.

By 2000, our corporate culture was beginning to shift, or as Deming might say, we were beginning to "put everybody in the company to work to accomplish the transformation." We had "adopted a new philosophy," and we had created "constancy of purpose." Furthermore, our four process platforms had given us the fractal-like patterns for developing all future process improvements.

Single source supply would not be fully fleshed out for another five years, but we were already *the only bottler in the world operating our DCs with zero inventory*, and not coincidentally, it was determined that we also had *the freshest product in the world*. Assets began melting away — we would soon be running 33% fewer trucks, selling excessive warehouse space, and days of inventory on hand would continue to drop despite the addition of SKUs and normal sales growth.

More importantly, the conceptual foundations and the leadership philosophies described earlier were becoming more established — but they were not yet well accepted by those managers and supervisors who felt as if they were losing control of their ability to command. Our processes were improving, but our culture had not yet been fully transformed. We had not yet learned how to nurture a collaborative process — we needed something profoundly different than managing people for results. Without collaboration our emerging systems could not be sustained.

Our Customer Information Center (CIC) further evolved out of this need for real-time collaboration. Most people at first thought CIC was just a call center for taking orders and processing complaints. We probably should have called it "Triple C" for "Customer Collaboration Center."

The CIC is open 24/7/365, and every TGW naturally creates the need for more new information. Likewise, new information could cause additional TGWs. For instance, suppose someone calls at 3:00 AM to say "I'm sick and won't be in today." The customer information center updates the human resources files (new information) and dispatches an alternative qualified associate to fill the position (more new information). What if your computer crashes? No problem; call the CIC about your TGW and they will dispatch a tech for you. If he can't fix it, he will call the CIC with the TGW. Sometimes these looping patterns of communication would result in the need for use of our 911 special cause platforms.

Everything we did and everything new that we developed self-referenced one of these four platforms. Everything seemed to emerge as a "just-like" reference to something else that had come before. The process was beginning to talk to itself — to self-organize — without the intervention of bosses to get things done.

Consequently, what now looks extremely complex was in fact analogous to the geometric growth of fractals, the division of cells in biology, or those birds that are so easily able to flock together. For instance, we developed the "Pop-Shop" — POP stands for "point-of-purchase" materials or signage in the lingo of shoppers. It was another "just-like" reference — If we could run distribution centers without product inventory, there was no reason to inventory point-of-purchase items. Why not make them (literally print them on demand) and cross-dock them with the Cokes? It was another example of "what could be," and we did it. New information would precipitate the design of new point-of-purchase and the Customer Information Center would enable our sales force to order customized signage for each customer's unique desires, ready for tomorrow's delivery to faraway distribution centers — "just in time." Again, we were the *first bottler in the world* to do this, and very few have this capability today. The Pop-Shop then emerged into a central supply system for everything we touched, from parts to paper clips. Literally everything was flowing seamlessly inside this process.

One person, more than any other, has maintained the discipline for maintaining these process platforms. His name is Steve Plumlee. Steve managed our information systems (IS) for more than 25 years.

Without Steve, this architecture would be just a blueprint. It is, in fact, a reality because it is embedded like DNA and permeates everything that has to do with our information systems. In other words, our information systems architecture is a "just-like" reference to our leadership philosophies, and, as a result, everyone is touched by it every day in some subtle way.

All this duplicity, synchronicity, and simplicity within both our operating systems and our information systems created what we have so often call "just-like" references, in everything we did. This in turn made both training and continual improvement far easier and much more intuitive.

"Constancy of purpose" in Steve's world means that we never strayed far from this disciplined information system architecture.

The *smart order* was merely a natural evolution of the continual improvement that followed the idea of *single source supply* and emerged from these four fractal-like platforms. The Pop-Shop, and countless other innovations, were just milestones along the way.

These four process platforms then became the backbone upon which all of our systems operated:

- **The Replenishment Process**
- **The New Information Process**
- **The TGW Process**
- **The Special Cause Process (911)**

Like everything else, the resolution of the dilemma regarding how our managers and supervisors were to move from a command and control structure to a process control environment emerged naturally out of what had come before. We were about to learn how to nurture this collaborative process — something profoundly different than managing people for results. We did not plan it; it was just another example of the emerging complexity that came from this fractal-like approach to continual improvement.

In Steve Plumlee's world, whenever we tell the system anything, it never forgets; so we can always data-mine practically any previous class of transaction. Here, "transaction" is not a "just-like" reference to accounting, as in "credits" and "debits." Instead, it is a "just-like" reference to *relationships*, as in "customers" and "suppliers." In this way, transactions that fire together literally wire together in a way that is analogous to the way we think.

By now, it should be clear that there are just four types of transactions (replenishment, new information, TGWs, and special cause) inside the kaizen model, and they always occur at the intersection of a customer and a supplier. Taken together, they document the history of our relationships throughout the *demand chain*.

This derivative capability allowed us to make operational the cliché, "Just ask why five times." There was no longer reason to assign blame or credit to a nearby associate. We could now collaborate with real-time data in order to continually improve the process.

In this way, as our information system's architecture continued to evolve, it self-referenced our operating processes, and out of this emerged the capability to provide what we called "after sales service." It became the fifth process platform. These five information system platforms are, of course, "just-like" references to our operating processes:

- **The Replenishment Process**
- **The New Information Process**
- **The TGW Process**
- **The Special Cause Process (911)**
- **The After Sales Service Process**

All aspects of these five platforms were welcome additions from the perspective of our *moment of truth* associates. Their tasks were becoming part of a more precise process, with clear direction that seemed to be constantly improving, and they had an easy way to report things gone wrong without blame. And, the 911 process seemed to bring much needed assistance before the job became "too much."

The exact turning point of acceptance for our managers and supervisors is difficult to pinpoint, but one conceptual trigger point does stand out.

Until approximately 2003, we routed separate people to the tasks of selling, ordering, delivering, and merchandising. In other words, our associates were specialists, working in separate silos and responsible only to "their" boss for "their" task on "their" route.

In the course of one week, multiple associates might visit any given customer for the various permutations of these tasks. Likewise, with issues like: turnover, paid time off, 24/7/365 operations, things gone wrong, and new information; it was extremely difficult to know who was actually on the route assigned to some particular individual — much less whether their boss was available at that particular time to handle the issues.

The blinding flash of the obvious came when we realized that we could quit routing individual people for specific tasks. Instead we could bundle the tasks to better accommodate individual customer needs. Then, we could create bus routes of these bundled tasks, and attach available associates with the necessary skills to do multiple tasks. We had dismantled the corporate silos and created a single source customer service model that looked very much like our kaizen model. The bundle of tasks (service requirements) for each customer became the constant and our people became multi-functional.

Thought about in this way, we could be flexible with the work force and consistent with our customer service, which was in turn tailored to the customer's needs. We were institutionalizing quality consciousness. We were, almost without knowing it, creating a process control environment. We were positioned to manage the process for improvement rather than managing the people for results.

We no longer needed specialized routes, because we could now bundle our service offerings customized for each unique customer and combine them on the same trucks. Our bus routes became *combo* bus routes.

This opened the door to flexible work schedules, part-time associates, and the ability to more easily work around the clock and around the calendar with staffing levels matched to our customers' requirements.

Our information system architecture worked better under this approach, too. And, our Customer Information Center could more easily assign associates with the necessary skills to established combo bus routes, and also manage vacation schedules and staffing levels. Logistics kept the routes balanced based on value-added time, and they had the capability to manage new information surges with our 911 capabilities, because the new information was known ahead of time.

Suddenly, our managers and supervisors were freed of mounds of administrative duties and the need for constant "fire fighting." They were, instead, armed with unbelievable amounts of process information. Everyone was finally accepting the transition from *command and control* to *process control*. Rather than blaming an associate for a TGW (like excessive returned product), our managers could now data-mine the transactions, ask why five times, determine trends, and solve customer problems in order to improve the process, rather than just blame some associate.

Soon, we found it possible to build loads accurately for every individual customer, including point-of-purchase materials and pictures for each unique "point of availability," and cross-dock it over 200 miles in less than 12 hours onto combo bus routes. And, we did this with precise new information for execution and real-time feedback of things gone wrong, which enabled us to continually improve the process and become better without "hammering" our people.

Looking back, as we implemented, improved, and evolved these five process platforms, we discovered and incorporated every aspect of the time paradigm in just over five years. We were operating around the clock and around the calendar with very fast cycle times and very high service frequencies, and we had eliminated countless non-value-added steps and significant inventory from our operating systems. These measures, together with our bus-route-like scheduling, had reduced common cause variation from our operations and resulted in much improved "on time in full" deliveries; and we were doing it with far fewer trucks.

The "single source supply" concept was fully fleshed out. It became our new "what is," and it was offered as a service to our neighboring bottlers. The Coca-Cola Company acknowledged this "best practice," copied it, and rolled out "parts" of it inside their own supply chain. The "inoperative" term here is "parts of it." You can't just pick and choose parts from a system that is holistic. The whole is always bigger than the sum of its parts, and it is the relationships that make this so. Nevertheless, imitation is still the sincerest form of flattery.

After that, it was just a matter of time before we added "the smart order" to our continually improving customer service capabilities.

This journey began suddenly when we became aware of systems thinking, but it developed slowly because of our limited appreciation of those cultural distinctions that metaphorically separate the cowboys from the Indians. As we began to realize that it was the *caring relationships* that allowed the *process* to become precise, we also became increasingly aware of the significance of *variation* in everything we do and the need to be open to new and improved paradigms as we let go of old beliefs that had served us so well before.

Nurturing new habits and protecting each other from our past points of view became essential to the continual improvement of our culture. Providing our managers and supervisors with real-time process measures was what finally enabled them to set aside their old habit of holding their people accountable for the results of the process. They were then able to focus their attention on improving the process — after all is said, you can't improve results; you can only improve the process. Today, our culture is what enables the process to improve. Before, it was what had inhibited us.

It is difficult to separate the principles that we refer to as our Sys-Tao leadership philosophy from the processes that made up our operating systems. It is always easier to explain concept before detail — principle before process — but life is lived the other way 'round. We experience the details first; then, as we listen, learn, and share, the processes evolve and become better, and we are then better able to comprehend the principles. This is what I have explained as emerging complexity. I call it Sys-Tao.

> *Tao is a principle. Creation, on the other hand, is a process. That is all there is; principle and process, how and what.*
>
> **– Lao Tzu**

We had indeed become better, and 2010 was our best year ever no matter how you measure it. Ask the Coca-Cola Company; they paid for these results. Ask our customers or our shareholders. Ask our suppliers or our associates. You can even ask our competitors. Better yet, come take a look for yourself. It is my hope that you will always be welcome at Great Plains.

So, I feel comfortable ending with this quote:

> *A leader is best when people barely know he exists, when his work is done, his aim fulfilled, they will say: we did it ourselves.*

— Lao Tzu

Some Concluding Thoughts

There are quite a few frequently asked questions that relate to this journey. Although the questions are different, the answers are pretty much the same.

The questions most frequently asked are what I would call "how-to questions." You know, questions like:

> How can a young person, starting out, apply this?
>
> How can a CEO best transform his company?
>
> How best can executives get their CEO to listen to this?
>
> How would I do it differently, if I were to do it again?

Deming would say there is no such thing as "instant pudding." That of course was before instant pudding was invented, but we can still understand what he meant.

My answer to these questions is that like so many things in life, you have to experience it to understand it. Just knowing the principles is not enough. It helps, but if you want to learn to swim you must jump in. The principles will make far more sense once you get wet.

Having said that, the single biggest lesson I learned based on my experience can be summed up with these words:

Collaborative Customer-Focused Systems Thinking

"Collaborative" goes to the notion of understanding relationships.

The more we try to understand causes and effects, the more we realize that we don't really understand; but the more we focus on relationships, the more we understand.

"Customer-Focused," when connected to the word "collaborative," profoundly changes the traditional role of management.

"Systems thinking," when modified by the words "collaborative customer-focused," shifts the emphasis from managing people for results to managing the process for improvement. This in turn underscores the need to measure the process, and creates the realization that the process cannot be controlled by "one brain." The process must take on a life of its own — it must self-reference and control itself. It can be improved by management, but only when there is customer-focused collaboration.

These words allow managers to become leaders whose primary role is to nurture the culture, improve the process, and set the strategic direction — the aim. When this is the case, an organization will have been transformed from a command and control structure to a process control environment.

Paradigms, habits, and the organization's cultural environment must all three become fluid — that is what continual improvement is all about, and it is management's job to allow it to happen.

One last question: "Is this Sys-Tao way of leadership replicable, and is it scalable?" I believe that it is, but a better question might be: "What if it is not?"

Changing paradigms, habits, and the cultural environment of larger more established organizations is of course more difficult, but more importantly, it is also a two-edged sword.

It is an obvious competitive advantage for the more nimble entrepreneurial start-up organizations that can do these things more easily, and it is clearly a threat to the larger more established organizations that believe it is neither replicable nor scalable.

Furthermore, because Sys-Tao is more like the way all living things are naturally organized, and because it is more like the way all living things have evolved, it seems reasonable that this type of emerging complexity will also have a lot to do with separating the winners and losers as organizations continue to evolve. I wonder what Darwin would say?

Epilogue

On December 30, 2011 we sold Great Plains to The Coca-Cola Company for $364 million, nearly 11 times the company's EBITDA (earnings before interest, taxes, depreciation and amortization).

Thirty-two years before we had invested $7.5 million and assumed $37.5 million in debt, in order to buy the company my grandfather bought 58 years before that.

Based on the $7.5 million investment we made in 1980, the average rate of return was about 13% for each of those 32 years.

Great Plains also paid after-tax distributions of $10 million for each of the ten years prior to the sale. Taking this into consideration the overall after tax return averaged about 13.4% and the after-tax cash generated was about $420 million.

So, why did we sell?

Faced with an aging senior management team and an increasingly diverse shareholder group, this increased liquidity and the assurance of consistent future cash flows just made sense. A conservative 3.3% after-tax return on proceeds of the sale would maintain the company's $10 million after-tax distributions into perpetuity, and deferring the sale just one year would have cost shareholders more than $32 million in increased capital gains taxes.

We had come full circle from where this story began, thirty-two years before. It just made sense, and it was once again the right time to sell the business.

Furthermore, for more than five years, The Coca-Cola Company had wanted to re-organize, re-structure, and re-engineer their existing business model with their bottlers. That 2006 front-page article in *The Wall Street Journal* is early evidence of this strategy (*see* **Appendix IV**). Their current plans to refranchise the bottler system are undoubtedly good ones, but the second and third effects of "harsh interventions" like these are always difficult to predict, and not something that fit our circumstances — in our case this provided further reason that it was a good time to sell.

To be successful in the long term this type of change will inevitably have to become reliant upon a more collaborative approach to systems thinking. To operate effectively at world-class levels, it must also be able to cope with things gone wrong in real time inside a seamless process, while responding to new information quickly and predictably — it must self-reference and control itself.

When this is the case, the system will have again begun the journey of creating relationships and always becoming better. It is the way all living systems naturally evolve, and this emerging complexity is the way continual improvement happens most naturally in the real world — it is the Sys-Tao way.

They bought our "Sys," but the "Tao" comes only with the people. The people of Great Plains will always have a bright future because they understand and I hope that this book has helped you better understand too.

> *The master in the art of living makes little distinction between his work and his play, his labor and his leisure, his mind and his body, his education and his recreation, his love and his religion. He hardly knows which is which. He simply pursues his vision of excellence in whatever he does, leaving others to decide whether he is working or playing. To him he is always doing both.*

> **– Zen Buddhist text**

Appendices

How Culture Molds Habits of Thought

Erica Goode

AUGUST 8, 2000

The New York Times Company

UNIVERSITY OF MICHIGAN

Dr. Richard Nisbett and his colleagues have found that people in different cultures think not just about different things, but think differently.

For more than a century, Western philosophers and psychologists have based their discussions of mental life on a cardinal assumption: that the same basic processes underlie all human thought, whether in the mountains of Tibet or the grasslands of the Serengeti.

Cultural differences might dictate what people thought about. Teenage boys in Botswana, for example, might discuss cows with the same passion that New York teenagers reserved for sports cars.

But the habits of thought — the strategies people adopted in processing information and making sense of the world around them — were, Western scholars assumed, the same for everyone, exemplified by, among other things, a devotion to logical reasoning, a penchant for categorization and an urge to understand situations and events in linear terms of cause and effect.

Recent work by a social psychologist at the University of Michigan, however, is turning this long-held view of mental functioning upside down.

In a series of studies comparing European Americans to East Asians, Dr. Richard Nisbett and his colleagues have found that people who grow up in different cultures do not just think about different things: they think differently.

"We used to think that everybody uses categories in the same way, that logic plays the same kind of role for everyone in the understanding of everyday life, that memory, perception, rule application and so on are the same," Dr. Nisbett said. "But we're now arguing that cognitive processes themselves are just far more malleable than mainstream psychology assumed."

In many respects, the cultural disparities the researchers describe mirror those described by anthropologists, and may seem less than surprising to Americans who have lived in Asia. And Dr. Nisbett and his colleagues are not the first psychological researchers to propose that thought may be embedded in cultural assumptions: Soviet psychologists of the 1930s posed logic problems to Uzbek peasants, arguing that intellectual tools were influenced by pragmatic circumstances.

But the new work is stirring interest in academic circles because it tries to define and elaborate on cultural differences through a series of tightly controlled laboratory experiments. And the theory underlying the research challenges much of what has been considered gospel in cognitive psychology for the last 40 years.

"If it's true, it turns on its head a great deal of the science that many of us have been doing, and so it's sort of scary and thrilling at the same time," said Dr. Susan Andersen, a professor of psychology at New York University and an associate editor at Psychological Review.

In the broadest sense, the studies — carried out in the United States, Japan, China and Korea — document a familiar division. Easterners, the researchers find, appear to think more "holistically," paying greater attention to context and relationship, relying more on experience-based knowledge than abstract logic and showing more tolerance for contradiction. Westerners are more "analytic" in their thinking, tending to detach objects from their context, to avoid contradictions and to rely more heavily on formal logic.

In one study, for example, by Dr. Nisbett and Takahiko Masuda, a graduate student at Michigan, students from Japan and the United States were shown an animated underwater scene, in which one larger "focal" fish swam among smaller fishes and other aquatic life.

Asked to describe what they saw, the Japanese subjects were much more likely to begin by setting the scene, saying for example, "There was a lake or pond" or "The bottom was rocky," or "The water was green." Americans, in contrast, tended to begin their descriptions with the largest fish, making statements like "There was what looked like a trout swimming to the right."

Over all, Japanese subjects in the study made 70 percent more statements about aspects of the background environment than Americans, and twice as many statements about the relationships between animate and inanimate objects. A Japanese subject might note, for example, "The big fish swam past the gray seaweed."

"Americans were much more likely to zero in on the biggest fish, the brightest object, the fish moving the fastest," Dr. Nisbett said. "That's where the money is as far as they're concerned."

But the greater attention paid by East Asians to context and relationship was more than just superficial, the researchers found. Shown the same larger fish swimming against a different, novel background, Japanese participants had more difficulty recognizing it than Americans, indicating that their perception was intimately bound with their perception of the background scene.

When it came to interpreting events in the social world, the Asians seemed similarly sensitive to context, and quicker than the Americans to detect when people's behavior was determined by situational pressures.

Psychologists have long documented what they call the fundamental attribution error, the tendency for people to explain human behavior in terms of the traits of individual actors, even when powerful situational forces are at work. Told that a man has been instructed to give a speech endorsing a particular presidential candidate, for example, most people will still believe that the speaker believes what he is saying.

Yet Asians, according to Dr. Nisbett and his colleagues, may in some situations be less susceptible to such errors, indicating that they do not describe a universal way of thinking, but merely the way that Americans think.

In one study, by Dr. Nisbett and Incheol Choi, of Seoul National University in Korea, the Korean and American subjects were asked to read an essay either in favor of or opposed to the French conducting atomic tests in the Pacific. The subjects were told that the essay writer had been given "no choice" about what to write.

But subjects from both cultures still showed a tendency to "err," judging that the essay writers believed in the position endorsed in the essays.

When the Korean subjects were first required to undergo a similar experience themselves, writing an essay according to instructions, they quickly adjusted their estimates of how strongly the original essay writers believed what they wrote. But Americans clung to the notion that the essay writers were expressing sincere beliefs.

One of the most striking dissimilarities found by the researchers emerged in the way East Asians and Americans in the studies responded to contradiction. Presented with weaker arguments running contrary to their own, Americans were likely to solidify their opinions, Dr. Nisbett said, "clobbering the weaker arguments," and resolving the threatened contradiction in their own minds. Asians, however, were more likely to modify their own position, acknowledging that even the weaker arguments had some merit.

In one study, for example, Asian and American subjects were presented with strong arguments in favor of financing a research project on adoption. A second group was presented both with strong arguments in support of the project and weaker arguments opposing it.

Both Asian and American subjects in the first group expressed strong support for the research. But while Asian subjects in the second group responded to the weaker opposing arguments by decreasing their support, American subjects actually increased their endorsement of the project in response to the opposing arguments.

In a series of studies, Dr. Nisbett and Dr. Kaiping Peng of the University of California at Berkeley found that Chinese subjects were less eager to resolve contradictions in a variety of situations than American subjects. Asked to analyze a conflict between mothers and daughters, American subjects quickly came down in favor of one side or the other. Chinese subjects were more likely to see merit on both sides, commenting, for example, that, "Both the mothers and the daughters have failed to understand each other."

Given a choice between two different types of philosophical argument, one based on analytical logic, devoted to resolving contradiction, the other on a dialectical approach, accepting of contradiction, Chinese subjects preferred the dialectical approach, while Americans favored the logical arguments. And Chinese subjects expressed more liking than Americans for proverbs containing a contradiction, like the Chinese saying "Too modest is half boastful." American subjects, Dr. Nisbett said, found such contradictions "rather irritating."

Dr. Nisbett and Dr. Ara Norenzayan of the University of Illinois have also found indications that when logic and experiential knowledge are in conflict, Americans are more likely than Asians to adhere to the rules of formal logic, in keeping with a tradition that in Western societies began with the Ancient Greeks.

For example, presented with a logical sequence like, "All animals with fur hibernate. Rabbits have fur. Therefore rabbits hibernate," the Americans, the researchers found, were more likely to accept the validity of the argument, separating its formal structure, that of a syllogism, from its content, which might or might not be plausible. Asians, in contrast, more frequently judged such syllogisms as invalid based on their implausibility — not all animals with fur do in fact hibernate.

While the cultural disparities traced in the researchers' work are substantial, their origins are much less clear. Historical evidence suggests that a divide between Eastern and Occidental thinking has existed at least since ancient times, a tradition of adversarial debate, formal logical argument and analytic deduction flowering in Greece, while in China an appreciation for context and complexity, dialectical argument and a tolerance for the "yin and yang" of life flourished.

How much of this East-West difference is a result of differing social and religious practices, different languages or even different geography is anyone's guess. But both styles, Dr. Nisbett said, have advantages, and both have limitations. And neither approach is written into the genes: Asian Americans, born in the United States, are indistinguishable in their modes of thought from European-Americans. (EMPHASIS ADDED BY BOB BROWNE)

Dr. Alan Fiske, an associate professor of anthropology at the University of California at Los Angeles, said that experimental research like Dr. Nisbett's "complements a lot of ethnographic work that has been done."

"Anthropologists have been describing these cultures and this can tell you a lot about everyday life and the ways people talk and interact," Dr. Fiske said. "But it's always difficult to know how to make sense of these qualitative judgments, and they aren't controlled in the same way that an experiment is controlled."

Yet not everyone agrees that all the dissimilarities described by Dr. Nesbitt and his colleagues reflect fundamental differences in psychological process.

Dr. Patricia Cheng, for example, a professor of psychology at the University of California at Los Angeles, said that many of the researchers' findings meshed with her own experience. "Having grown up in a traditional Chinese family and also being in Western culture myself," she said, "I do see some entrenched habits of interpretation of the world that are different across the cultures, and they do lead to pervasive differences."

But Dr. Cheng says she thinks that some differences — the Asian tolerance for contradiction, for example — are purely social. "There is not a difference in logical tolerance," she said.

Still, to the extent that the studies reflect real differences in thinking and perception, psychologists may have to radically revise their ideas about what is universal and what is not, and to develop new models of mental process that take cultural influences into account.

Dr. Nisbett is also featured in the video, *West and East, Cultural Differences* (Sys-Tao.org), already referenced in Chapter Four: *Cultural Roots, West Meets East.*

GAAP vs. Thruput Accounting

Traditional accounting practices known as GAAP (Generally Accepted Accounting Practices) allocate overhead, depreciation, labor, and yield losses to the ingredients of a perfect Coke and come up with a figure known as COGS, "Cost of Goods Sold." Net sales minus cost of goods sold is what they call gross profit. Gross profit is difficult to calculate, and it is of little use from a customer's perspective. It is useful mostly for evaluating past performance from the company's perspective. It is a number created more for Wall Street than for Main Street. Consumers don't drink allocated expenses.

A perfect bottle of Coke is made up only of the bottle, the secret formula, and the cap. That is it. The cost of this perfect bottle of Coke includes no overhead, no depreciation, no labor, no yield losses, and nothing else other than the perfect Coke that a satisfied consumer uses to quench her thirst. That is what we call Product Cost. It is easy to calculate, because it is nothing more than the recipe, the bill of materials that makes up a perfect Coke. It is easy to understand, and easy to account for. You don't have to be an accountant to understand a perfect Coke; in fact, it is easier to understand if you are not an accountant. Net sales minus this recipe for "product cost" is what we call *thruput*.

Thruput is a larger number and a simpler concept than gross profit. It is not burdened with cost allocations. It is simply the cash money coming into the company whenever we sell Cokes, and it is an objective measure of how much customers value Cokes over time.

The following chart compares a GAAP financial statement with a thruput accounting financial statement:

Generally Accepted Accounting Principles (GAAP) include non-cash calculations (depreciation and amortization) in the calculation of both cost of goods sold (COGS) and in selling, general, and administrative expenses (SG&A), so it is necessary to add these expenses back to GAAP operating income in order to get earnings before interest, taxes, and depreciation (EBITDA) which is exactly the same thing as cash operating profit (COP . . . it is just harder to understand for most people.

The Income Statement Simplified

GAAP	Thruput
Net Sales	Net Sales
–COGS	–Product Costs
Gross Profit	Thruput=Customer Value
–SG&A	–Total Cash Operating Expense
Operating Income	EBITDA=COP
+ Depreciation	–Depreciation
+Amortization	–Amortization
EBITDA=COP	Operating Income

COGS=cost of goods sold
SG&A=selling, general & administrative expense
EBITA=earnings before interest, taxes, depreciation, and amortization
COP=cash operating profit

GAAP operating income is another one of those numbers mostly useful on Wall Street. To get to GAAP operating income from thruput accounting simply subtract the non-cash items (depreciation and amortization) from the COP.

GAAP accounting allocates some of the total operating expense (TOE) and some of the non-cash items to products. That is why GAAP cost of goods sold (COGS) is a bigger number than thruput accounting's product costs, and that is why gross profit masks thruput, our measure of customer value over time.

Allocating total operating expense and non-cash items to products or services can also cause us to needlessly raise prices and reduce services which will in turn result in less Thruput over time.

In this way, these GAAP allocations can be both confusing and misleading for operating managers who are focused on decisions affecting the future.

GAAP is more descriptive of what has already happened ("what was") from a shareholder point of view, but it is less predictive of how future decisions might affect both shareholders and customers ("what could be").

The ramifications of these differences become quite clear when considered in the context of *breaking even*.

GAAP selling general and administrative (SG&A) costs are generally thought of as fixed expenses while cost of goods sold (COGS) are considered to be expenses that are variable with net sales. The point at which the sum of these fixed and variable expenses are equal to net sales is considered to be the "break-even point."

As shown below, as you move to the right of this break-even point, volume increases — the gap that opens up represents *profits* — and, as you move to the left the gap represents *losses*.

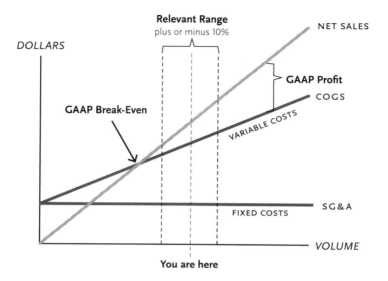

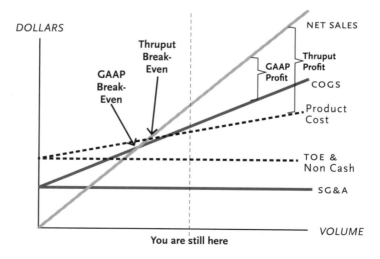

Unlike GAAP accounting, thruput accounting does not absorb (allocate) anything. As a result, *variable costs* are reduced when compared to GAAP. The cash differences like labor and yield losses are captured in the total operating expense. The total operating expense plus non-cash items like depreciation and amortization then make up the *fixed cost* line, which is higher when compared to GAAP. As a result, the *break-even point* moves to the right and changes in volume have far more effect on both profits and losses, as shown below.

At the other extreme, some companies use *activity based costing* (ABC) in order to more "accurately" track "costs." Terms like "cost to serve" or "direct marketing expenses" are often quantified and moved from the *fixed cost* line and allocated to (absorbed in) the *variable cost* line. This, of course, has the exact opposite effect of thruput accounting. The *break-even point* moves to the left and changes in volume have far less impact on both profits and losses. All three of these options are shown in the next illustration.

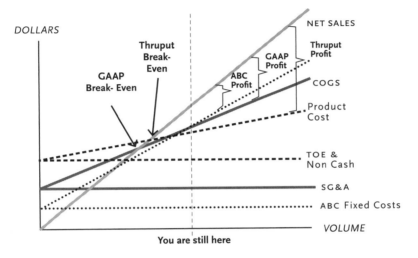

Most economists agree that in the long run all costs are variable. They may be right in some macro way, but in terms of our definition of "economic paradoxes," the "apparent facts are in conflict with the models or theories" that look too far into the future. In the near term and in the relevant range (+/- 10% from where you are now) most costs other than Thruput Accounting's "Product Costs" are in fact fixed.

The more costs are allocated, the higher variable costs are "assumed" to be and the lower fixed costs are "assumed" to be. Thruput Accounting does not allocate costs. GAAP does and ABC does a lot. They are just different versions of the truth, and they are very different paradigms.

Which model to choose is, of course, debatable, but the implications of that choice are not.

> • **The more costs are allocated:** The Break-Even Point moves to the left creating a reduced sense of concern regarding lost Volume.

> • **The more costs are allocated:** There is less sensitivity to the need for customer service and Quality Consciousness.

• **The more costs are allocated:** There is more sensitivity to pricing and the perceived need for Revenue Management.

• **The more costs are allocated:** There is more reason to be risk averse and conservative regarding competitive pricing.

• **The more costs are allocated:** Opportunities for eliminating Waste are less obvious, because they are less visible.

• **The more costs are allocated:** Opportunities to increase Capability are viewed with less interest because incremental Volume is less appreciated, and the Fixed Costs are perceived to be lower than they actually are.

GAAP works well for Wall Street, but it is both confusing and misleading on Main Street.

APPENDIX III

(Referenced on page 54)

The Parable of Deming's Red Beads
&
The Funnel Experiment

There have been many books and countless articles written about the works of W. Edwards Deming. Some of the books are listed here:

Aguayo, *Dr. Deming, The American Who Taught the Japanese About Quality*; Fireside, New York, NY, 1990

Delavigne and Robertson, *Deming's Profound Changes*; PTR Prentice Hall, Englewood Cliffs, NJ, 1994

Deming, *Out of the Crisis*; Massachusetts Institute of Technology Center for Advanced Engineering Study, Cambridge, MA. 1986

Deming, *The New Economics for Industry, Government, Education*; Massachusetts Institute of Technology Center for Advanced Engineering Study, Cambridge, MA. 1993

Scherkenbach, *Deming's Road to Continual Improvement*; SPC Press, Knoxville, Tennessee, 1991

Walton, *The Deming Management Method*; Perigree Books published by The Putnam Publishing Group, New York, NY, 1986

These books describe Deming's 14 points, his system of Profound Knowledge, and Statistical Process Control in a more straightforward and academic way than what has been shared in this case study of Great Plains Coca-Cola.

Also Included in these writings are two classroom exercises that Deming used to illustrate many of his management principles. Each of these exercises deals directly with the effects of variation on a system.

The Parable of the Red Beads focuses more on the adverse psychological effects of traditional management techniques while The Funnel Experiment illustrate the effects of "tampering" with a stable process

In my opinion, Rafael Aguayo's book, *Dr. Deming, The American Who Taught the Japanese About Quality*, provides the best explanation regarding these two exercises that so persuasively cut to the chase of what is wrong with our traditional leadership philosophies.

What follows are excerpts from his book:

CHAPTER FIVE

Dr Deming, The American Who Taught the Japanese About Quality

VARIATION IN MANAGEMENT

(The Parable of Deming's Red Beads)

. . . Let's put ourselves in the shoes of a manager confronted with a typical problem at the end of the year. It seems reasonable to believe that if everyone worked a little better or harder, the group would be better off. One way in which many executives feel this might be accomplished is to provide incentives by rewarding exceptional individual performance and punishing below average results. This is the idea behind merit pay and incentive pay, but we find it in all aspects of our society — grading, for instance.

It's promotion time and Mr. A is reviewing the results of his group. His company measures performance by the number of defects produced per quarter. Naturally, fewer defects indicate better performance. Below is a table with the results for the six individuals in the group, along with their ranking for the year.

Defects per Worker per Quarter

Name	Quarters				Total	Rank
	1	2	3	4		
Ken	8	10	12	9	39	5
Barbara	6	4	11	7	28	1
Lenny	11	11	11	8	41	6
Noboru	8	11	8	11	38	4
Cathy	15	5	12	4	36	3
Steve	5	9	9	10	33	2

The results are straightforward and objective. Mr. A doesn't like subjective ratings because they are too "unscientific," but he knows how to analyze performance by ranking people from first to last. This year Barbara was the star performer and Lenny was the worst, with an unacceptable level of 41 defects. In no quarter did Barbara's level of defects exceed Lenny's. Barbara is in line for a promotion to manager. She certainly earned her merit pay. Lenny, on the other hand, appears to have been goofing off. Whatever the reason, his work wasn't good enough. Some organizations would let him go. Imagine what the group could do if it had five more people just like Barbara.

THE RED BEAD EXPERIMENT

One of Deming's best-known lectures is his Parable of the Red Beads. Using a simple example, he is able to demonstrate much of what is wrong with American management.

In a typical session Deming asks for volunteers from his audience. He needs six willing workers, no experience necessary. The company will train them. After some coaxing, six members of the audience step forward. Now some additional personnel are needed to ensure quality. Two inspectors are recruited. The only requirement is an ability to count to twenty. Finally, a chief inspector and a recorder are chosen. Deming acts as foreman.

Six workers, one foreman, and an administrative staff of four are now about to mimic a typical work environment. This is a modern factory employing the latest and best in management methods. The factory makes white beads. But some times it turns out red beads, which are defects. The customers pay only for white beads.

The production equipment includes two plastic rectangular pans. One is larger than the other and contains 4,000 beads, 3,200 whites and 800 reds. A rectangular paddle with fifty holes is part of the equipment. The paddle is dipped into the beads and, when raised, should be filled with beads. Preferably white beads. A very concerned management has established a factory goal of only two red beads per paddle.

Deming, acting as the serious foreman, demonstrates the production technique. "Pay attention. I want everyone to pay attention," he begins. "There is no variation in the method; therefore there should be no variation in the results. Grab the larger container in the right hand and slowly pour the beads into the smaller container. Now grab the smaller container in the right hand and pour the beads back into the larger container. Now angle the paddle and immerse it into the beads so that it's fully submerged and draw it out. Careful, don't shake it."

After drawing the paddle out, he points out eight red beads among the fifty it holds.

"As you can see, I intentionally made a few red beads so you can see what they look like. Now walk over to the inspectors and show them your paddles. Each inspector counts the number of red breads. The chief inspector compares his count with the other two inspectors. If there are no discrepancies, the chief inspector announces the count."

"Eight," is announced by the chief inspector

"Now dismiss the willing worker."

"Dismissed."

"Very good. We do everything wrong in this company," Deming says, "except one thing. The inspectors are independent."

Now the willing workers begin their training with one practice run apiece. As they proceed, Deming shouts slogans and cliché's one would expect from a crusty foreman.

"Not that way, you weren't watching me. Like this!"

"Don't shake the paddle, just angle it out."

"We want only the best workers. We constantly strive for improvement."

"There will be no quitting. You can be fired but you can't quit."

After the foreman has trained his workers, he asks for an average worker. Ken volunteers to be the average worker.

"Good. Now Ken is our average worker, and he'll go first. Everyone else is above average."

Ken begins his first day's production under the watchful eye of our foreman. He pours the beads from one container into the other.

"Don't tilt it. Weren't you watching me? That's better."

When he finishes, the chief inspector announces the count.

"Eight. Dismissed."

"Well, Ken, I suppose that's not too bad for a first try, but you're going to have to do better."

Next Barbara tries her hand. She produces six red beads on her first try. Our foreman booms out,

"Now, Barbara made only six red beads. If she can make only six, no one should make more than six."

Lenny on his first try produces eleven, Noboru makes eight, and Cathy makes fifteen, producing an outcry from our foreman.

"Now hold on a minute. Cathy, don't you understand? Weren't you paying attention? That kind of performance just isn't acceptable. Our goal is two red beads at the most and you're not even close."

Steve on his turn produces five red beads.

After the first quarter a performance review is conducted.

"Steve was our best worker. He gets the highest pay increase and earns merit pay. He's in line for a promotion. Poor Cathy, we all like her but she can't do the job. She's not living up to her ability. We may have to let her go."

And so it goes for three more quarters. Each quarter a personnel review is conducted, and each quarter a different individual is at the top and a different individual is at the bottom. But the overall results don't change much. Deming gets to utter every cliché known to man, dumps on a worker whenever his or her red bead count is very high and praises him or her whenever it's very low. At the end of four runs the results are as follows:

Full Year Results

Name	Quarters				Total	Rank
	1	2	3	4		
Ken	8	10	12	9	39	5
Barbara	6	4	11	7	28	1
Lenny	11	11	11	8	41	6
Noboru	8	11	8	11	38	4
Cathy	15	5	12	4	36	3
Steve	5	9	9	10	33	2
Total	53	50	63	49		

The results are exactly those first used at the beginning of this chapter to demonstrate a performance review. Of course, from the nature of the red bead production technique we know that the performance of each individual on any given day and, in fact, for any length of time is due entirely to chance. But what is surprising is the amount of variation from person to person. The best quarterly performance in our experiment is four red beads, repeated by both Barbara and Cathy while the worst is fifteen by Cathy in the first quarter.

We all acknowledge the existence of chance in everyday life. Yet most of us assume that chance is not responsible for differences in individual performance. But here we encounter a situation where chance is responsible for 100 percent of the difference in performance. Surprisingly, in many commercial situations where one might believe that the individual controls the results, all or almost all the variation from person to person and from quarter to quarter is due to chance.

Let's return to Deming's demonstration. The results for the four quarters are in, and the foreman who has been complaining about quality and touting management's commitment to quality throughout the year now has a tough task to face.

"Management has asked me to inform you that although you improved, it was not enough. We were prepared to close the plant but someone in management has come up with a brilliant idea. This is a stunning breakthrough in management technique. We'll keep the plant open with the three best workers. All the above-average performers will stay on, while the laggards will be let go. Barbara, Cathy, and Steve will stay on. As for Ken, Lenny, and Noboru, we're sorry. We all like you. Please pick up your last paycheck as you leave."

The best workers must do two runs each. On her first run Barbara produces eight red beads and on her second try thirteen. Cathy makes fifteen and thirteen. Steve has eight then seven. Using the best workers, the plant has sixty-four read beans, the worst quarter ever. Of course, we knew that there was no reason for the plant to operate any better or worse using the best workers. The three workers were chosen because they were the best workers in the past, but management should be interested in the future. However, when all the variation in performance is due to chance, past performance is neither a guarantee nor an indication of future performance.

The management of the bead factory held the workers responsible for their individual production. They blamed the workers for the problems of the system. The following memo taken from a Navy yard bulletin aptly demonstrates this kind of mistaken thinking.

> I want to reemphasize that improved quality of work is critical to every one of our jobs. True productivity should translate into increased production of an acceptable professional product. Shoddy work does not improve productivity no matter how quickly [sic] or in what quantity it is completed. We would only discredit ourselves and disserve the public by turning out poor quality work.
>
> The importance of the concept of accountability of individuals, and the power of a pervasive human knowledge among the workers, supervisors, managers and that each individual will be held accountable for his work products cannot be overstressed. Audit trails must be maintained that document completed work. People generally want to do the right thing, but in a large organization they frequently don't really understand what is the right thing. Management must make crystal clear what is expected from each employee and that personal performance is essential to holding a job or being promoted. When instructions and expectations are made absolutely clear, and follow-up action is taken swiftly where failures occur, compliance will result. Proper managerial conduct will result in a loyal, highly motivated, and very capable work force with tremendous surge of capability. The managerial ability to pull all of this together in a manner that supports human development is a vital ingredient in our shipyards. We should intensively and analytically evaluate how to handle compliance (holding workers, supervisors, and managers accountable) and to deal with failure in a manner that will have the highest payoff in improving quality and productivity.

How do we know whether or not the differences are due to chance?

When management looks at information on output or performance, it is confronted with a bunch of numbers. The usual assumption is that each number is due to one specific cause, such as the effort or lack of effort of an individual. But in a system like the bead factory, all the variation is due to chance, which means that it is caused by the system not the workers. Management is responsible for the system. Why then blame the workers?

How do we determine if the variation in a system is due to chance or individual causes?

CONTROL LIMITS

In the bead factory the average number of red beads per person is nine. The upper control limit and the lower control limit calculated for the red bead factory are respectively eighteen and one. As long as the number of read beads on each tray is between eighteen and one and there are no trends in the data, we are confident in saying that all the variation from person to person is due to chance. In other words, the variation is inherent in the system and will persist no matter who the workers are.

The idea behind the control limits is fairly simple. When chance is responsible for all the differences in a measured quantity, such as production output or the number of defects, almost all of the data will fall within three common measures of variation (standard deviation) from the average...When all the data fall within the control limits and there are no trends or cycles, we have achieved what is called statistical control or stability. All variation is best explained by chance.

When, however, a point falls outside the control limits, either above the upper limit or below the lower limit, then it is worth our while to hunt for the cause of the variation. Anything that causes a point to fall outside the control limits is probably a special cause. Special causes can be found and often eliminated.

A system that is operating in a state of statistical control is not necessarily defect free. In the red bead factory, for instance, the average level of defects was more than 18 percent. But what it does mean is that at this point there can be no further improvement by looking for individual causes of defects. Only by working on the whole system can we achieve improvement. The system must be altered in some fundamental way, and that only management can do.

A PRACTICAL EXAMPLE OF STATISTICAL CONTROL

Although the term may seem imposing, we all have some familiarity with the idea of achieving statistical control. Suppose for instance, you are assigned the task of starting a completely new department. At first everything seems chaotic. Every problem is new and special. To deal with the problems and day-to-day tasks you establish routines and procedures. As you learn to handle a certain type of situation, it becomes routine, and can be easily delegated.

Gradually most of the special problems are eliminated and things begin to run smoothly. New situations are constantly cropping up, but much of the business on hand is handled in a routine fashion.

No business can operate for long unless a certain amount of stability has been achieved. Deming estimates that, based on his experience, in most business situations 94 per cent of the problems are problems of the system while only 6 per cent are special in nature.

SOME COMMONLY PROPOSED SOLUTIONS . . .

Hold the workers accountable for their work

Sounds wonderful. But the workers are helpless to improve. They haven't chosen the equipment, the suppliers, the lighting, the order of the tasks, or the layout of the plant. Changing the workers may have no effect on the results in a stable system. Workers are constrained by the existing system. Working twice as hard, if that were possible, would have no effect.

Merit reviews, incentive pay

Once again sounds wonderful but this will only cause strife and tension. If all the workers were to have their pay doubled, the results would not change. Some workers will of course perform "better," that is to say; he or she will have fewer red beads. Giving them higher pay will not improve quality but will cause resentment among those who do not receive incentive pay. Holding a lottery and giving the winners more money may be harmless, and even fun, but call the results of a lottery merit and deep trouble will result . . .

Let the workers compete against one another

Competition in this and analogous situations is totally inappropriate and harmful.

New technology, automation, mechanization

Suppose someone convinced the board that the problem lay in lazy and inefficient workers. After much research and analysis, management purchases new mechanical dippers, which would replace the workers. But quality does not improve. It stays the same or deteriorates while a host of new problems has to be dealt with. Many companies that embraced automated plants as their solution to problems of quality and productivity are quickly retreating from them.

Quotas, piecework, work standards

Quotas double the cost of production. Quotas may result in more items being shoved out the door, but the cost to the company increases as returns increase. As quality declines, inventory increases, waste soars, and the customer's perception of the product quality declines.

But quotas have a more insidious characteristic. If everyone is meeting the quota, someone must be capable of exceeding it on a given day. But once she reaches the quota, she stops for fear that the quota will be raised. It is not unusual to find workers stopping an hour before the whistle blows. Great peer pressure is exerted to keep production down so that all can meet the quota. No one make suggestions that will improve production. The workers in such an environment are unhappy, but from managements point of view the quota is being met and that is all that counts.

Meeting specifications, conformance

The goal in the red bead parable is two red beads at most. How was this decided? At a meeting someone looked at the results and decided the firm could do better. A goal was set as a target. In other words, like most goals, it was invented. Is it possible to meet the goal? Only by working outside the system. Outside of bribing the inspectors, however, most workers are bound by the system.

Everyone doing his best: working harder

Everyone is already doing his or her best, working his or her hardest.

Excessive testing of new employees

In this system there will be problems regardless of who the employees are. If the employees all had IQs of 200 and were master craftspeople as well, it would make no difference. They are all constrained by the capability of the system.

Management by walking around

Just imagine all the damage that can be done by allowing bright young individuals who are ignorant in the nature and sources of variation walking around the plant floor, or office, and making changes and suggestions on the basis of three-minute observations. In the next chapter we will cover the harm that can be done by constant changes to a system.

WHAT WILL HELP

In our bead factory nothing can be done at the factory level to improve quality. Neither the workers nor the foreman are capable of making the necessary changes. Even the quality control expert might be helpless if he does not have the authority to change policy. Holding the workers, the foreman, or the quality control expert responsible for quality would be futile and senseless.

The problem's source is the supply of beads. If we could eliminate all the red beads from the incoming source, we would eliminate all the red breads from the end product. The problem begins well upstream from the factory. But why are so many red beads being delivered. It could be for any number of reasons. The specifications may call for no more than 20 perfect defective beads being delivered, which guarantee exactly 20 perfect defective beads being delivered, which guarantees exactly 20 perfect defectives.

The supplier may have been chosen on the basis of lower price, without much regard for quality. Management may be on a cost-cutting binge or just unaware of the effect on the bottom line of inferior quality.

It's possible that the supplier's production method produces 20 percent red beads but that a few modifications may eliminate all red beads. The company should join forces with the supplier, sharing knowledge to improve the supplier's production methods.

The changes necessary to improve the quality of the incoming materials are changes in policy that only management can authorize.

COMMON CAUSES

When all the special causes of problems and variation have been eliminated and statistical control or stability has been established, variation and problems will still exist. The variation at the point is said to be caused by common causes.

Common causes are interactive in nature. Let's consider a hypothetical example. Suppose we have a plant assembling a flywheel that will rotate at very high speeds during operation. Each worker arranges three plates on a rod. Now in the real world every plate is not totally uniform; variation exists, and every plate has one section that is slightly heavier than the rest. The difference is very small and can't be seen or felt without sophisticated equipment. But if the heavy parts of all three plates are aligned, the flywheel will wobble at high speeds and have a greater tendency to fail.

Most of the time, the heavy sides of each plate are aligned in different directions so that they counterbalance. But once in a while, strictly by chance, the three plates will be perfectly aligned and the mechanism will fail. The failure is not caused by any single cause but rather is a chance occurrence of the system. Several factors have to occur for the failure to occur. Plate 1 *and* Plate 2 *and* Plate 3 have to be aligned, and the mechanism has to be spinning at high speeds for a long period of time. No matter how hard you searched for a cause of the breakage, you couldn't find one. Everything in the system is working as it should. The workers place the plates on the rods in exactly the same manner for the mechanisms that fail and for those that don't. The plates and rods are equally good in each case, but every once in a while, strictly by chance, a mechanism that is prone to failure will be produced. The same system that produces the good products produces the bad products in exactly the same way.

Management, through their words and actions, act as if there were two systems working side by side — one producing good products and one producing defects. Management often acts as if all the good products are produced by the system when everyone does his or her job while defects must be caused by someone doing something different, outside of prescribed fashion. As a result, they are quick to take credit for success but blame those working in the system for failures. But this attitude not only causes friction and dissension with their own work force, it also prohibits improvement because their view of the cause of problems and failures is inaccurate.

Often times when a failure or problem occurs, the organization is sent into a frenzy searching for the cause. One tire manufacturer had all the day's defective products segregated and stored in a room until their engineers could dissect all the defectives and search for the cause of failure. This was the case for years, with the level of defectives remaining the same.

A CURE FOR THE PROBLEM

Let's suppose the engineers of our hypothetical plant producing the flywheel figure out the random alignment of the heavy sides of all three plates could cause the mechanism to become unstable when spinning at very high speeds. How could they prevent further failures from occurring in the future? One way would be to determine the bias of each plate, using sophisticated equipment, before it is assembled onto the rods and mark the heavy side with a red dot. The workers would then be instructed to assemble the mechanism so that the red dot on each plate is turned 120 degrees clockwise from the one before it.

Another method would be to inspect all the finished, assembled mechanisms for any wobble by testing each one at high speeds before it is sent out. In both cases the cost of eliminating a possible failure would be very high, requiring extensive inspection, new procedures, and new equipment.

But suppose, on the other hand, the company is constantly improving quality by lessening variation. The company works with the supplier of the plates and constantly strives to make the plates more uniform by improving the platemaking process. In time the plates become so uniform that, even if all three are perfectly aligned, the wobble even at high speeds is minimal. The problem goes away without being attacked directly. And the cost is not higher and may be less.

COMPARING THE TWO METHODS OF IMPROVING QUALITY

These two methods of improving quality, one by inspection and the other by constant improvement of the process and the products, highlight the difference in attitudes and understanding between conventional companies and those companies that have taken Deming's lessons to heart. The companies that rely on inspection to improve quality believe that quality is expensive (because of the way they believe improvements are made). The Deming companies, on the other hand, are constantly improving the process and the product without justifying every improvement, confident that higher productivity, lower costs, and higher profits will result.

A Real Life Example: Nashua Corporation began applying quality control to the manufacture of carbonless paper in 1979. Before the institution of quality control, their production process was marked with many interruptions for adjustments. While the process was running, technicians would take samples of the paper and make tests to determine if the quality of the copy was satisfactory. When the mark was too dark, or too faint, the process would be stopped to readjust the amount of coating being applied. When quality control was applied, the control charts indicated that the process was in fairly good statistical control. Some special causes of variation indicated by the control charts were tracked down and eliminated.

Realizing the nature of the remaining variation, the engineers then experimented with different settings and different formulations for the coating and brought down the amount of coating needed by 17 percent, resulting in a cost saving of more than $800,000 yearly, all with better quality. Improvements continued to be made very year thereafter, with quality improving and substantial cost savings accruing.

TWO KINDS OF MISTAKES

In analyzing variation there are two kinds of mistakes we could make:

1. We could mistake the cause of variation as being special in nature, when in fact; it is random and caused by the system (common causes).

2 .We could mistake the source of variation as being systemic in nature (common causes), when in fact; it is special in nature (a special cause) and can and should be identified and, if possible, eliminated.

If you ignore a new rattle in your car, continue driving, and the crankshaft breaks, you have made a type two mistake. If the quality in your plant or office is gradually getting worse, and you ignore it, you may be committing a type two error. When a new employee enters the work force and the number of mistakes of the department increases significantly, that may be a special cause due to the employee not knowing his job. If management disregards the problem, they are committing a type two error. Incidentally, who is responsible for making sure the employee is properly trained for his new job? That is management's responsibility

Type one errors are more common. Ask most managers at plants that are experiencing difficulty how many of the problems are due to the workers and the answer is almost always, "All the problems are caused by the work force." Soviet leader Mikhail Gorbachev made a type one mistake when he blamed a blast in a gas pipeline on the lax behavior of the workers. He blamed the workers at the nuclear plant at Chernobyl as being the culprits in the nuclear disaster there. When top management blame every accident on the lax behavior of the workers, they are admitting their ignorance and abdicating their responsibilities. It is not really clear that improper training or lax behavior is the cause, but it is almost certain that we are confronting common causes. If the training of everyone is indeed at fault, it is only management that can institute the proper training system wide.

Our Federal Aviation Administration tracks down the "cause" of every airline accident and ends up blaming someone or something for every accident.

At most companies, customer complaints are individually tracked down and brought to the attention of the individual thought to be responsible. One firm began drawing control charts of customer complaints after taking a Deming seminar and realized they had been chasing phantom problems for years. All their efforts in the past had been wasted. More importantly, now that they understood the nature of common causes, they were in a position to make genuine improvements.

One plant manager told Deming "Our engineers never rest until they have found the cause of every defect." According to the plant manager, quality control was not needed because they understood every problem. But for years the level of defectives had remained the same, a sure sign that defectives were due to common causes.

The plant engineers were wasting their time and probably making things worse.

The reader may protest, "Perhaps they were wasting their effort but no real harm was done." But there is another surprise in store. Chasing down phantom problems may do great damage. In fact, a perfectly good system can be ruined by over adjustment and trying too hard. To understand this, we have to examine some additional properties of a stable system.

CHAPTER SIX

Dr Deming, The American Who Taught the Japanese About Quality

STABLE SYSTEMS
(The Funnel Experiment)

I mentioned in the previous chapter that adjusting or interfering in a stable system instead of improving it could do considerable damage. Let me show you how with a simple mechanical system first demonstrated by Lloyd Nelson, the 1987 winner of the American Deming Prize. All we need are a funnel, a stand, a ball small enough to pass through the funnel, and a square piece of carpet at least two feet by two feet.

The funnel is mounted on the stand with its nozzle a few inches off the ground. We mark a large X in the center of the carpet and aim the funnel at it. We then drop the ball through the funnel, observe where it stops, and mark and measure that spot. Our objective is to have the ball end up right in the center of our target. We drop the ball through the funnel fifty times with the funnel stationary and mark the final resting place each time.

Let me tell you what I observed when I tried this. Once in a while the ball stopped on or very near the target, but most of the time the ball rolled off in one direction. The marks indicating the final resting spot of the ball formed a rough circle. A picture of what this looks like after five hundred drops is shown in Figure 5-1. When I did it for fifty drops, all but one point was within seven inches of the target and that point was nine inches from the target. If we were to keep trying, we would see the blank areas of the circle filled.

This is a stable system. It is in statistical control with no special causes of problems. The markings are randomly distributed, and if we tried to predict whether on the next try the ball would end up north or south of the target, we would have a one-in-two chance of being right.

ATTEMPTS AT IMPROVEMENT — MODEST ADJUSTMENTS — RULE 1

Let's try to improve our accuracy and get more of our drops closer to the target. No one is going to blame us for trying. In fact, in the real world a boss or a board of directors may be looking over our shoulder. Almost invariably we're asked what we're doing to improve results, and from experience we know we had better have an answer.

One possible solution is to adjust the funnel, whenever we miss the target, by an amount equal to the miss but in the opposite direction. If the ball ends up south of the target by two inches, we will move the funnel two inches north of its present position for the next attempt. Our reasoning is that with this adjustment the ball would have hit the target on the last try.

Let's call the first method with the funnel stationary Rule 1 and our new procedure of adjusting the funnel Rule 2, or the rule of modest adjustments.

Now we retry the experiment, making modest adjustments whenever we miss. The results for five hundred tries are shown in Figure 5-2. What has happened? The results are worse! Once again the scatter of the marks forms a rough circle, but the radius is larger. When I tried it for fifty drops, most of the points fell within ten inches of the target but one point was thirteen inches from the target.

Once again the system is in statistical control, but now the area of the circle is roughly double the area of the previous one, when we did nothing.

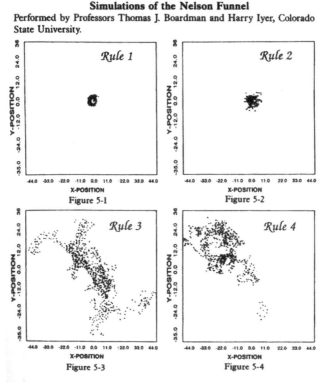

Simulations of the Nelson Funnel
Performed by Professors Thomas J. Boardman and Harry Iyer, Colorado
State University.

EXAMPLES FROM REAL LIFE OF ADJUSTMENTS USING RULE 2

Let's look at some real-life situations where modest adjustments like those we just performed are done as a matter of course. You may find these examples funny or disturbing, but keep in mind that the people performing or authorizing the adjustments are completely unaware of the ill effects of their actions.

EXAMPLE I. In the military it is common practice to test a gun in the morning. If the target isn't hit, then the gun or the sighting mechanism is readjusted so that it would have hit the target on the last try. Does this improve the accuracy or lessen it?

Prior to seeing the results of modest adjustments of the funnel, most of us would have answered automatically that adjusting helps the accuracy. But remember there are many things that can cause a gun to miss its target. Each bullet has a slightly different shape. The gunpowder in each bullet is packed differently. Constantly changing air currents could cause a difference in the bullet's trajectory. There are untold sources of variation. Adjusting after one shot is doing exactly what we did when we adjusted the funnel each time it missed the target.

If you're like me, this example is hard to swallow. All of us have adjusted something to bring it back in line. We have taken it as a matter of faith that this would make things better. But the lesson here is that it does not; it only makes things worse if the system is stable. If you don't believe it, try it yourself.

But there is another point to consider. When some American observers went to Japan to find out the Japanese secret, they came back disappointed because the only difference they could find was the Japanese penchant for boisterous singing in the morning. Objective observers will only see what they're trained to see. Few people would notice that certain things *aren't* done. Subtle differences will be completely overlooked if one isn't aware of their importance.

But let's look at some other situations where modest adjustments are taking place.

EXAMPLE II. William W. Scherkenbach, who studied under Deming at NYU and is now in charge of statistical methods at General Motors, investigated a mechanism that guaranteed that a part would be made to specifications. The mechanism worked all right. But when he shut the mechanism off, he found that everything was still made within specifications but with less variation, closer to the ideal. In other words the quality was better and the costs were lower with the mechanism turned off.

EXAMPLE III. In the example of the previous chapter Nashua was doing the same thing manually, but with a modified form of our rule for modest adjustments. They didn't adjust their mechanisms after every miss, only when the miss was "large enough." But the results were the same. They were making the system worse by over-adjusting.

EXAMPLE IV. A manager looks at the sales figures for his group. He's elated to see that almost half his staff performed above average last year, undoubtedly due to his superior leadership and management skills. Unfortunately, about half are below average, and there are a few laggards in the bottom 15 perfect who haven't responded to his leadership.

To help the laggards and encourage the super achievers, he sets up an incentive program. Anyone selling over a certain dollar amount next year will earn a bonus. Anyone selling below a certain level is penalized.

Of course next year some will earn the bonus and some will be penalized, but will the company be better off or worse off because of this merit system?

EXAMPLE V. The Federal Reserve Board is charged with regulating the nation's money supply. It looks at current data on the money supply or inflation, depending on what it is trying to regulate this year, and decides that money supply is "too high" or "too low" and takes steps to compensate for the amount it is off target.

I think if you're reading this for the first time, it must be a bit of a shock to realize that some of our best efforts to make things better are making things worse. But wait, there's more.

RULE 3 — MORE EXTREME ACTION

Clearly there is a lot of adjusting going on in business, but our funnel experiment suggests much of this effort makes matters worse, rather than improves it. But let's go back to the funnel and try something else. Perhaps we weren't trying hard enough with Rule 2. Let's try some other rules to see if we can't improve upon the results.

We can devise a new adjustment procedure, which we'll call Rule 3, or the rule of extreme adjustments. Now we'll move the funnel relative to the target instead of relative to its last position. Using our new rule, if the ball ends up three inches south of the target, we move the funnel to a position three inches north of the target for the next drop. Under Rule 2 we would have moved the funnel three inches north of its previous position. The results for Rule 3 are shown in Figure 5-3.

Remarkably, the results are worse than ever. The system is exploding in two directions, getting progressively worse. It is no longer stable. We have taken a perfectly good system (that was stable) and through our efforts to make it better (less variable) made it much worse, to the extent that it is now unstable. The situation is getting out of control. To keep the system from exploding, we have to shut it down.

When we tried modest adjustments, we took a system that had a certain level of natural variation and through our efforts to lessen the variation increased it. In effect we added another source of variation, our movement of the funnel. But the variation we introduced by moving the funnel didn't cancel the natural variation of the funnel. Instead it combined with it, giving us a system with greater variation. But with the extreme adjustments of Rule 3 the variation is cumulative, gradually pushing the results farther and farther from the target

Let's look at a few cases of Rule 3 . . . extreme adjustments:

EXAMPLE I. A company's personnel policy calls for it to pay competitive salaries. Each year it orders a survey of compensation for its industry and adjusts its pay scale so salaries are 10 percent higher than industry average. One-year sales and profits decline. The company looks at its personnel expense and decides it's too high. The policy is now changed so that salaries are 10 percent below the average. When the economy turns around, it finds itself short of people. It reverts to its old policy.

EXAMPLE II. The federal government collects money through various revenue collecting measures, including the federal income tax. It redistributes money back to the states in the form of revenue sharing based upon a formula negotiated in Congress---the idea being to help those areas of the country that are poorer (or below average). In the past the formula favored the South and Southwest because the median income of those areas was below that of the Northeast. During the 1970s the Northeast became one of the nation's most distressed areas, and the formula was changed so that funds would flow back into the Northeast and away from the South and Southwest.

Senators and representatives from outside the Northeast are now complaining that the system is unfair because incomes in the Northeast are among the highest in the nation. The more they try to make it "fair," the more unfair it seems to become.

In general, shifts in policy based on results are examples of the rule of extreme adjustments. Rather than stabilizing the situation, these frequent and extreme adjustments make the situation more volatile and more "unfair."

RULE 4 – JUST LIKE THE LAST

So far our efforts directed at obtaining better results haven't been successful. For better results we could substitute other phrases, such as greater accuracy, more fairness, greater uniformity, or fewer defects. However we describe the desired result, the Nelson funnel has helped us see the folly in several courses of action. But we can try one more rule.

In our final attempt we devise Rule 4, which I'll call the rule of just like the last. Under this rule we re-aim the funnel after each drop so that it is directly over the spot where the previous drop ended up. The results for five hundred tries using Rule 4 are show in Figure 5-4.

If you weren't totally discouraged before, this should do the trick. Now the system is exploding in a manner similar to the situation under the rule of extreme adjustments, but in just one direction.

Lets look at some examples of Rule 4 . . . Just Like the Last Adjustments:

EXAMPLE I. Most of us at one time played a game called Telephone or Post Office. Someone starts by whispering a message into the ear of the adjacent person. That person in turn whispers the same message into someone else's ear. After passing this way through thirty people, the message is completely transformed. Every third of fourth person in the chain heard a different message.

EXAMPLE II. The chain of command is an example of Rule 4. Whether communications are flowing up or down the chain of command in an organization, after going through five different people, the original message and intent are altered. The message after twelve people may be just the opposite of the original.

This example makes a strong case against management systems with many levels. When it comes to layers of management, less is more. It also indicates that pushing the level of authority and expertise closer to the scene of the action cuts down on the amount of misunderstanding and leads to better results.

EXAMPLE III. A devastating example of Rule 4 is worker training worker. A worker comes on the job and is told to learn from another. After three weeks she's an old-timer, a pro. When someone new comes on the job, she is told to teach him. Soon the new worker is also a pro. Each has a different idea of what the job is. Some will admit not really knowing what the job is. None is properly trained. If everyone has a different idea of what the job is, how can quality possibly be achieved? Think back to the number of jobs you've started in a new company or department where one person was responsible for training everyone. I doubt most of us will remember many instances. But I'll bet almost everyone who has held a job was told at least once, "You'll pick it up," or "Learn from those around you."

Some firms have all kinds of teaching materials and manuals but much of it is incomprehensible. Whose obligation is it to see that workers are properly trained? Management's.

EXAMPLE IV. Rule 4 was followed when a Japanese car manufacturer sent DuPont a paint sample with instructions to match it. When the batch was used up, they sent a sample of the new batch of paint to DuPont with instructions to match this batch. They continued ordering and using paint in this manner. After a while a noticeable difference developed between the first batch and the most recent.

To assure the same color, the manufacturer should have left a sample of the original batch with DuPont with instructions to match the original whenever more paint was required.

EXAMPLE V. Legal precedent is an obvious but frightening example of just-like-the-last adjustment. Each judge interprets a case based on her understanding of the law. Her decision is then the platform from which other judges interpret the law. Their decisions then serve as the basis for future decisions. After a while a law can be interpreted in a way that is unrelated to its original meaning.

EXAMPLE VI. Languages are another example of Rule 4, just like the last. After several hundred years American English had developed many distinct accents and drawls. National television, on the other hand, has brought the accents of the various regions much closer together, since children now learn to speak English as much from television as from the parents. International television will undoubtedly bring the English spoken in the various English-speaking nations much closer together.

REAL IMPROVEMENT

With all these attempts at improvement backfiring, you've got to wonder if there is any way we could improve the results. The answer is, yes, there is, but not by constant adjustment. The urge to do something, to do anything, can make things worse if one proceeds in ignorance.

Only changes of the system, not adjustments of the existing system (which is already in control), can lessen variation and volatility. Change the funnel, the length of the funnel's barrel, the ball, the size or texture of the ball, the surface on which the ball lands or any combination of these, and you change the system. These changes are all fundamental changes to the system. Not all changes in the system will make things better. The only way of being certain is to try it — on a small scale, if possible.

Over-adjustment of a stable system invariably makes things worse. This deserves a special name — tampering. There are three ways of acting on a stable system. One is a change in the system leading to improvement, the second is a change in the system making things worse, and the third is tampering, which also makes things worse. Only one of the three, a change in the system leading to improvement, will make things better. Only management is in a position to make any of the changes, but making changes in the system without the benefit of profound knowledge can result in tampering — worsening, even ruining, a system.

But remember, when we say a system is stable that means there is variation. Some systems can have a lot of variation and some display little, but all systems vary.

The funnel may be a lot of fun to play with, but the reason it's being used here is that the conclusions we draw based on our experiment with the funnel hold true for any system in statistical control, whether the system is mechanical or human.

An example of tampering in a human system is when someone is overseeing the work of or second-guessing someone who is perfectly capable of doing the job correctly. Have you ever been in a situation where the inspector or boss knew less than you? You knew the job, knew what had to be done, and were perfectly capable of doing it, but you had to get your work checked out or approved by the boss. There are few things as demeaning. Basically the firm is telling you that in their eyes you're incapable of doing the job; you're an idiot, or incompetent or can't be trusted.

TAMPERING IN A SMALL SYSTEM

Having someone look over your shoulder when you're perfectly capable of doing the job robs you of pride of workmanship. It's demeaning and will worsen the output. You develop the attitude, "Well, the supervisor will catch the error anyway, so why bother."

The supervisor develops the attitude of, "I know his or her work is good. I really don't have to look it over." Neither person has a job; the results are worse than with someone doing the job unsupervised.

Some inspectors in such a situation give themselves a job by finding problems that don't exist. This is even more extreme tampering, making things progressively worse. One experience of this kind is enough to make most people swear off corporate America. I think that's one reason why we have so many entrepreneurs in this country.

The situation is completely different if a worker is incapable of doing the job. The worker who hasn't yet mastered the job should be supervised and helped. A worker may be new to the job, in which case he should be trained, he may be an experienced worker whose work has fallen out of statistical control, in which case he is in need of special help; or his work may be in statistical control, but unsatisfactory, in which case he should be reassigned and taught new skills.

When a worker whose work was formerly acceptable deteriorates below the lower control limit for the group, it indicates he is in need of special help. But management shouldn't blame him. Fault is not the issue. Solutions and improvement are. Management should consider this as information about the system's shortcomings, which they can use to improve the system for everyone who works in it.

It is a fact of life that people's performance can decline. Management has to be able to distinguish which of the workers are really in need of special help and which just have a tray filled with more red beads than average. The former is a special case and can be addressed; the latter is due to chance, and trying to address it directly will only make things worse. You had better have some way of distinguishing one from the other.

Control limits and knowledge of variation are the best ways we have of making that distinction. Once management determines who is in need of special help, they have an obligation and a responsibility to provide that help. They have a chance and an opportunity to help one worker improve his output, which in turn raises the output of the group and in the process, bolsters the morale of everyone in the company

WRONG WAYS OF DEALING WITH VARIATION – TAMPERING 101

Let me tell you of some of the funny ways we humans have of dealing with variation when we don't really have the answer, or in some cases the question. Deming tells of a plant that was consistently producing a high level of defects. Using the information on hand, he drew a control chart and calculated the average defect rate of 4 percent, an upper control limit of 6 ½ percent, and a lower control limit of 1½ percent.

All week-to-week data were within the control limits, indicating that the system was stable, but with a high defect rate.

Showing this to the manager, he asked what measures the manager felt were appropriate to improve the situation. The manager proceeded to redraw the control limits, making them narrower and lower.

Would redrawing the control limits change the reality of the system? Of course not. Would it change anything? Yes, it could make things worse. It could lead to the mistaken assumption that stability hadn't been reached, leading one to mistake common causes of defects for special causes. This could lead management to interfere when it wasn't appropriate, or, once again, tampering.

ANOTHER EXAMPLE — TAMPERING COURSE 102 Dr. Joyce Orsini, a respected consultant who obtained her doctorate under Deming's guidance, told me the following all too typical story. One perpetual problem among bank tellers is the daily differences between the cash they should have according to the accounting records and the cash they actually have at the end of the day. They may end up with more cash or less cash than indicated by the books. Normally the difference is quite small, although occasionally the amount is substantial. This is a common and persistent problem in all banks.

A chief executive of a New York bank noticed the problem and decided he would eliminate it the old-fashioned way. He just wouldn't tolerate it. He issued an edict that any teller with more than two differences a month would be placed on probation. Any teller on probation for three months would be terminated.

Most of the differences disappeared. The chief executive was elated. He reported the results to his board along with an explanation of his form of management. All that was necessary, according to him, was for him to put his food down and not accept errors. The board of directors was also elated. This was obviously sound management. But why tolerate two differences a month? No one could think of a good reason, so the rule was changed. Just one difference placed a teller on probation. All the differences disappeared.

How could differences disappear so quickly and so completely? In fact, a simple but sophisticated system had been developed by the tellers to deal with the problem that management denied existed. The tellers began operating their own pools of money when the new policy was initiated. When overages occurred, instead of being reported, they were saved. When a teller came up short on given day, he would withdraw from the funds saved on the days he was over. Those who needed funds borrowed from those with excess funds. A sophisticated system of borrowing and lending had evolved.

This was, of course, contrary to the bank policy, but it was the only way of surviving in the bank. Everyone in the bank knew of the existence of these pools of funds except management. Whenever management uses fear, they will get incorrect numbers and misleading information.

This went on for ten months before management discovered its existence. The president was enraged and took it out on middle management. For weeks life was hell for them.

But who was really responsible? Simple knowledge of variation indicated that day-to-day differences were in statistical control. No special causes were at work. Only changes in the system could improve the performance of the tellers as a whole. The workers were powerless to (improve) make any changes in the system. They could not change the lighting, the room temperature, the time between breaks, or the monotony of the job. They could not change or improve the training, the frequency of job changes, or any other significant aspect of the system. Only management could make these changes. But management had abdicated its responsibility because of ignorance.

SYMPTOMS OR CAUSES?

In both of the above examples we can categorize the position of management as one of ignorance of the nature and sources of variation, perhaps even of the existence of variation. But another way to look at their action is to realize that they were dealing with the symptoms of the problem and responding to them, rather than dealing with the causes of the problem.

But the causes of common problems cannot be attacked directly. It is a mistake to believe that one is improving quality when an inspector recognizes and rejects a defective product or when a major quality flaw is found. That is just recognizing a defect being produced in the system. It is not improving quality. It is not improving the system.

LOVE THOSE PROBLEMS

Every system has some problems. Someone is busy solving these problems. Problem solving is fun, it gives many people meaning, and the results are measurable. "I solved fifteen major problems this week." "Without me the plant would have shut down." "I saved the company a lot of headaches by stopping that shipment." When there are lots of problems, people can easily measure their value to the company. Problem solving is necessary, no doubt about it. Good problem solvers are important. But solving all the problems that come up does not improve quality. The source of the problems is left intact when we recognize defective products and prevent them from reaching the customer.

Improving the operation and lessening the number of problems that are created by the system doesn't have the instant gratification associated with problem solving. A lot of thinking and study of theory and current circumstances is often required. Improvements are sometimes small. But improvements, large or small, are cumulative. In a short while there are fewer day-to-day problems. Improvement can be a threat to many people. People who are busy solving problems will become threatened by improvement and resist it. Their attitude is understandable and justified if management maintains an us versus them attitude and views people as commodities to be discarded when their present job categories become obsolete.

The problem is compounded when people are judged based on how many problems they solve. Anyone who takes the time to truly improve the system lowers not only his own rating but the rating of everyone in his group as well. He not only will put himself out of work but will hurt his peers as well.

A company that operates using fear, positioning top management against workers and middle management against both, cannot produce the continual improvement in quality necessary to compete in the marketplace.

A SHORT COURSE IN STATISTICS

Let's consider variation in a different context. Imagine that we recruit fifty people who have tested very high on some test, say an IQ test. We sit all of them in a room and give them another standardized test. We then rank them from one to fifty, based on the results of that test. Twenty-five of these people are below average for this group. So what? Are they in need of special help, or is this just another case of the red beads? How could you tell? One could draw a control chart and calculate control limits, although on just one test even this would carry some risk. It is unlikely that twenty-five individuals are in need of special help. Most likely this is just another red bead example.

But all too often it is assumed that those below average or those in the bottom 10 percent have done something wrong. A merit system, for instance, may reprimand, punish, or place on probation those who are in the "bottom 10 percent" of the work force. Reprimand the bottom 10 percent and you'll quickly destroy their self-image. Do it on a regular basis and you'll quickly destroy the morale of the group. Eventually, almost everyone ends up at the bottom at some point. Will reprimanding the bottom 10 percent make them achieve any better in the future? No! But it will destroy teamwork and any chance for improvement. No one is going to help someone else when doing so may help put the other person ahead of him in the review and give the helper a bigger chance of ending up in the bottom of the group.

The president of a well-known business school beseeched his faculty: Please help those students who are below average do better so they can also be above average. Some corporations only hired the top 10 percent of the graduating class of M.B.A.'s. As Deming says, "They got what they deserved."

The Nuclear Regulatory Commission spends extra time monitoring those nuclear plants that are below average. Historians rank our presidents every ten years or so. Last time, they made a startling discovery. Half of our presidents were above average. Lucky for us. Imagine if all had been below average.

In placing special regulatory emphasis on those plants that are below average the Nuclear Regulatory Commission is tampering. If the faculty complied with the request of the president of the business school, and gave special help to those below average, they would be tampering. Harmless tampering? Isn't it better to do something, do anything, than to do nothing? Acting without knowledge, particularly profound knowledge can quickly ruin a perfectly good system.

One part of profound knowledge is obvious to children but not to some college presidents. In any group, close to half will be below average.

IMPROVEMENT AND EFFORT

Asking people who work in a system to do better without providing a plan by which this can be accomplished will do no good. If they could improve quality or profits by 10 percent without a plan, they would already have done so.

A corporation is a highly interactive environment and the results in one area impact on many other areas. Asking everyone to work harder will not help results. The system has to be worked on, people have to work smarter not harder, and that requires intense cooperation. It requires equal cooperation of those in the "top half" and those in the "bottom half" without distinction, because there is no real distinction.

But one of the problems with existing management systems is that they destroy the very teamwork and cooperation that are absolutely essential to improvement. Those companies and those societies that cooperate most effectively in the complex industrial environment of today will see the greatest improvements in productivity and quality. Cooperation is one of the key ingredients of improvement. With cooperation everyone wins — all the employees, the customers, and management — so it is called win-win. But what is most often practiced in the United States are systems of extreme differentiation, where for every winner there is at least one loser, so they are called win-lose systems . . .

(Referenced on page 127, 165)

THE WALL STREET JOURNAL

Front page article, MARCH 12, 2006

Soda Rebellion

A Suit by Coke Bottlers Exposes Cracks in a Century-Old System

Serving Wal-Mart Is at Issue, But Spat Shines Spotlight On Local Businesses' Role

The Brownes' 84-Year History

BY CHAD TERHUNE

OKLAHOMA CITY – The black-and-white photos hanging in Robert Browne's office recall happier times for the longtime Coca-Cola bottler.

In a 1922 image, his grandfather stands proudly' in front of his newly acquired Coke bottling plant. A 1978 snapshot shows three generations of Mr. Browne's family celebrating a new contract with Coca-Cola Co. alongside Donald Keough, later Coke's president.

Yet last month Mr. Browne sued Coke. The suit by him and 54 other independent bottlers also named one giant Coke bottler, Coca-Cola Enterprises Inc. It seeks to bar them from breaching a century-old tradition at the iconic soda company, in which the indepen-

Robert Browne

dent companies that put its beverages in bottles and cans also deliver them to grocery stores and stack them on the stores' shelves.

Thirst Aid

Share of U.S. sports-drink market by volume, 2005

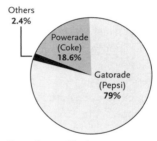

Others 2.4%
Powerade (Coke) 18.6%
Gatorade (Pepsi) 79%

Source: Beverage Digest

The problem: Wal-Mart Stores Inc. wants one Coke-produced beverage, the sports drink Powerade, sent directly to its warehouses.

Coca-Cola Enterprises has agreed to do so, within its own sprawling territory.

Smaller bottlers wouldn't be affected immediately. Yet they fear this is an opening wedge, a shift that ultimately could threaten their survival. Their concern is that straight-to-warehouse delivery will prove pleasing to Wal-Mart, that other chains will demand it, and that it would inexorably spread to other drinks and bottlers. The small bottlers then would see their close relationships with grocers diminished, and local marketing would suffer. Those relationships are the main way the bottlers feel they can drive sales in their territories—and thus their own business success.

Agreements dating to 1899 give Coke bottlers exclusive rights to handle sales and distribution within their territories, all the way down to building displays in grocers' aisles. Coke must rely on the bottlers, as well, to manage a growing assortment of new drinks and to execute marketing promotions. As a result, Coke's growth has always been built on a symbiotic relationship with local bottlers.

But Coke has also chafed at their independence, and the company has steadily nibbled away at it. Bottlers numbered more than 1,000 in the 1930s in the U.S. In the 1980s and '90s Coke encouraged consolidation, eventually shrinking their number to 76 nationwide. Now, Coke is also facing a stubborn slide in U.S. sales of its flagship Coca-Cola Classic as consumers buy more bottled water, expensive lattes and energy drinks.

Coke's, world-wide volume growth was 4% last year, down from a recent peak of 9% growth in 1997. In the U.S., the largest soft-drink market, Coke Classic sales are off 10% during the past five years and Coke's market share or the $68 billion-a-year soft-drink industry, is at a nine-year low. Coke's stock, trading in the low $40s, is well off its 1998 peak of nearly $89.

As Coke tries to reverse the slippage and boost new noncarbonated drinks, some Coke executives, and analysts believe the fragmented bottling network is a relic that must change. They depict the lawsuit plaintiffs as family-run businesses clinging to the past. Meanwhile, giant grocery retailers are aggressively pushing for ever-tighter efficiency in their supply chains. If Coke is to turn itself around, some maintain, it must gain better command of all the tentacles of its business.

"Coke is going back to control, control, control," complains Mr. Browne, chairman and chief executive of Great Plains Coca-Cola Bottling Co. "Their goal is getting rid of us munchkins."

The head of Coke's North American business, Donald Krauss, says Coke isn't trying to get rid of bottlers but can't ignore shortcomings in its business model. "It's about having one system that operates in concert." he says. "We can't keep having internal debates where 20 bottlers want to do it, this way and another 35 bottlers want to do it that way. I don't' think we can grow unless we adapt to how the customer landscape has changed."

The sides are squaring off in federal court in Springfield, Mo., with plaintiffs claiming the plan for direct-to-warehouse delivery is a breach of contract and defendants saying it is permitted. The bottlers that are suing handle nearly 10% of Coke's U.S. volume in bottles and cans. A hearing on a preliminary injunction against the warehouse plan is scheduled for later this month. That's just before 'Coca-Cola Enterprises, which handles 77% of Coke's volume in the U.S., begins delivering Powerade to Wal-Mart warehouses April 1 in its U.S. territory. (A pilot program is under way in Texas.)

Long History

Coke bottling got going in 1899 when two young Tennessee lawyers visited Asa Candler, an Atlanta businessman who had acquired the soda formula from the inventor, John Pemberton, and made it a popular drink at soda fountains. Mr. Candler didn't see a future in selling it in bottles, given the needed investment in equipment and workers. Though he doubted the two lawyers, Benjamin Thomas and Joseph Whitehead, would succeed, he gave them a bottling franchise for most of the U.S. with the price of syrup at a dollar a gallon in perpetuity.

They did succeed. A blend of the

home office's innovative mass marketing and relentless promotions by bottlers made Coke ubiquitous. Bottlers who'd been recruited by the Tennessee lawyers plastered the countryside with billboards and giant ads painted on barns. Many bottlers amassed fortunes and became benefactors of their communities, providing money for football scoreboards and other causes. Sales of Coke concentrate, similar to syrup, became Coke's primary revenue source.

Coke executives have worked ever since to undo the generous 1899 terms. The last time a majority of U.S. bottlers sued Coke was 1920, when the company first tried to charge more to cover a rising price of sugar. A settlement gave Coke some latitude to do so. Then in the 1980s and '90s Coke managed to shrink the number of bottlers by buying some of them, merging them and selling off majority stakes in the combined entities—a strategy known as the "49% solution" under legendary Coke CEO Roberto Goizueta. The selloffs were a source of rich Coke profit growth in that era.

One bottler Coke put together, and then took public, was Coca-Cola Enterprises. It has grown into a company with 73,000 employees and 2005 revenue of $18.71 billion in North America and Europe. Coke owns 36% of it.

In 2004 Coke got its first CEO who had been a bottler, Neville Isdell, who'd spent more than half his career in bottling overseas. He gave senior jobs to other veteran bottling executives. But he also has demanded better execution from the bottlers and said Coke will stop holding back on concentrate-price increases in some markets around the world because bottlers financial health has improved. Recently, he told investors that

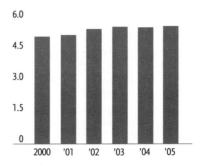

Not Much Fizz

Coke's beverage sales in U.S. and Canada, in billions of cases.

Source: the company

"our ability to respond to customers in the franchise system has not been what it should be."

The Browne family has been bottling, Coke in Oklahoma ,City since Mr. Browne's grandfather, Virgil. Browne, Sr., bought, the local franchise 84 years, ago. The elder Mr. Browne earned a reputation, as an innovator, becoming one of the first to sell Coke bottles in a six-pack.

His grandson Robert, now 63, worked summers at the plant as a teenager throwing glass bottles on the filling line. After college be worked as a consultant in New York, but returned to the family business at age 30, concerned that it might vanish in a wave of consolidation. "I always had it in my blood." he says.

He relished representing Coke in his community, sponsoring the state fair and Oklahoma traditions such as the annual Redbud Classic half-marathon. After the Oklahoma City bombing in 1995, he lent a Coke warehouse to the Red Cross. Like many bottlers, the Browne family grew wealthy selling Coke. Also like other bottlers, the family gained wide control over the key center aisles of supermarkets and how they featured Coke products.

In 1978, Mr. Browne agreed to an amended contract giving Coke more leeway in pricing concentrate. Coke, would use the extra money it took in to bolster marketing, it told bottlers, arguing that the company and its bottlers needed to join forces against rival PepsiCo Inc.

In the mid-1980s, Mr. Browne had a chance to buy the Coke bottler in Tulsa. Coke said it would approve the deal if Mr. Browne signed a new master contract it was championing, allowing unlimited increases in concentrate prices. Mr. Browne signed and kept expanding, adding territories in Oklahoma and Arkansas. In 2005. his company's revenue was $270 million, up nearly 7% from a year before. It's the seventh-largest U.S. Coke bottler, with about 1% of Coke's U.S. volume.

To improve service, to big customers, Mr. Browne built a sophisticated system for delivery to stores. It starts at his two bottling plants, where thousands of bottles and can roll off the line every minute. In a warehouse, workers called pickers assemble pallets of drinks for delivery. The drinks go to grocers in relatively small and, frequent deliveries that he believes reduce waste and offer better service.

Most of the 89 Wal-Mart stores in his territory get deliveries twice day, seven days a week. Mr. Browne is working with Wal-Mart on a system that would let him access its checkout-sales data as often as every 15 minutes so he can feed its stores with still more precision. Wal-Mart accounts for about a third of his sales.

Other employees of the bottler visit Wal-Marts three times a day to put the drinks on shelves and set up displays. At a store in Oklahoma' City recently, they built a tower of one-liter bottles of Vault, a new citrus soda from Coke. If they run out of products or get a complaint about a vending machine, they punch into handheld computers the code TGW, for "things gone wrong," plus a note to the person who needs to fix the problem.

The Wal-Mart Factor

About 10% of Coke's U.S. sales flow through Wal-Mart, analysts say. Wal-Marts all across the U.S. get their Coke products from regional bottlers that deliver to individual stores. But the giant retailer last summer sought to break with that tradition, asking to have Powerade sent to its warehouses, instead or stores, in areas where Coca-Cola Enterprises is the bottler.

Smaller bottlers say they were blindsided. They say Coke and its biggest bottler should have brought them into the talks earlier and sought their blessing. Coke's Mr. Knauss says the company and Wal-Mart discussed the idea with smaller bottlers as early as last July, telling them Wal-Mart wanted to make Powerade a stronger No.2 to Gatorade, which has nearly 80% U.S. market share. The owner of Gatorade, PepsiCo, bought the drink in 2001 and continued with a system of delivering it straight to warehouses.

"Wal-Mart is saying we want a consistent lineup of products in every store at the same price," Mr. Knauss says. "It's fairly hard for Wal-Mart or Kroger to run a national program under the "current way we go to market."

As part of the deal with Coke, Wal-Mart committed to giving Powerade more shelf space. Coke and Coca-Cola Enterprises say other retailers are also interested in having Powerade sent to their warehouses, but that it's too early to talk about delivering drinks besides Powerade this way. The second-largest U.S. bottler, Coca-Cola Bottling Co. Consolidated in Charlotte, N.C., also wants to deliver Powerade to Wal-Mart warehouses rather than stores, and is seeking to join the suit in support of Coke and Coca-Cola Enterprises.

For Wal-Mart, traditional store delivery frees up labor and offers other benefits, says a spokesman, Kevin Thornton, But the giant retailer has developed an elaborate distribution system that allows it to "know in real time how much product we have left and when we need to order new product," Mr. Thornton says. The warehouse-delivery plan "will allow us to apply that inventory management to Powerade. Doing this with Gatorade proves this business model works."

Coke introduced Powerade in 1994. The standard contract with bottlers said that, except for food-service. accounts, such as restaurants or airlines, the sports drink shall not be warehouse delivered by Coke. It didn't say anything about such delivery by bottlers. The suing bottlers cite a 1997 letter a Coke lawyer sent to the bottlers' association that said in part: "We believe the Powerade form of [master distribution, agreement] already does deny bottler warehouse delivery, but based upon discussions with your committee, we all agree, that the prohibition should be explicit."

Mr. Browne acknowledges that, if Wal-Mart gives Powerade more shelf space, sales of Powerade are likely to increase. But he says any problems of distribution or half-empty shelves can be solved within the existing system, noting that his own Powerade sales at Wal-Mart leapt 45% last year. Accusing Coke of caving in too easily to a retailer request, he says, "If someone calls up and says put more sugar in the Coke, are you going to do that, too? Coke is giving everything away."

Mr. Browne has a 28-year-old son, Web, working at the bottling company, as well as a 32-year-old daughter, Cory, who's a corporate lawyer. He wants to keep the Coke business in the family for a fourth generation. "I don't have a for sale sign in the yard," Mr. Browne says.

Internet Links to the Sys–Tao website

Sys-Tao.org

Bibliography

Aguayo, Rafael. *Dr. Deming: The American Who Taught the Japanese About Quality*. Secaucus, NJ: Carol Pub. Group, 1990. Print.

Bragg, Steven M. *Throughput Accounting: A Guide to Constraint Management*. Hoboken, NJ: John Wiley & Sons, 2007. Print.

Capra, Fritjof. *The Tao of Physics: An Exploration of the Parallels Between Modern Physics and Eastern Mysticism*. Berkeley: Shambhala, 1975. Print.

Capra, Fritjof. *The Web of Life: A New Scientific Understanding of Living Systems*. New York: Anchor, 1996. Print.

Christensen, Clayton M. *The Innovator's Dilemma: When New Technologies Cause Great Firms to Fail*. Boston, MA: Harvard Business School, 1997. Print.

Christensen, Clayton M., James Allworth, and Karen Dillon. *How Will You Measure Your Life?* New York, NY: Harper Business, 2012. Print.

Delavigne, Kenneth T., and J. Daniel. Robertson. *Deming's Profound Changes*. Englewood Cliffs, NJ: PTR Prentice Hall, 1994. Print.

Deming, W. Edwards. *The New Economics for Industry, Government, Education*. Cambridge, MA: Massachusetts Institute of Technology, Center for Advanced Engineering Study, 1993. Print.

Deming, W. Edwards. *Out of the Crisis*. Cambridge, MA: Massachusetts Institute of Technology, Center for Advanced Engineering Study, 1982. Print.

Dispenza, Joe. *Breaking the Habit of Being Yourself: How to Lose Your Mind and Create a New One*. Carlsbad, CA: Hay House, 2012. Print.

Goldratt, Eliyahu M., and Jeff Cox. *The Goal: A Process of Ongoing Improvement*. Great Barrington, MA: North River, 1984. Print.

Johnson, H. Thomas. *Relevance Regained: From Top-Down Control to Bottom-Up Empowerment*. New York: The Free Press, 1992. Print.

Johnson, H. Thomas, and Robert S. Kaplan. *Relevance Lost: The Rise and Fall of Management Accounting*. Boston, MA: Harvard Business School, 1991. Print.

Kahneman, Daniel. *Thinking, Fast and Slow*. New York: Farrar, Straus and Giroux, 2011. Print.

Kaplan, Robert S. and Robin Cooper: *Cost & Effect: Using Integrated Cost Systems to Drive Profitability and Performance*. Boston: Harvard Business School Press, 1997. Print.

McGilchrist, Iain. *The Master and His Emissary: The Divided Brain and the Making of the Western World*. New Haven: Yale UP, 2009. Print.

Nisbett, Richard E. *The Geography of Thought: How Asians and Westerners Think Differently...and Why*. New York: Free, 2010. Print.

Pink, Daniel H. *Drive: The Surprising Truth About What Motivates Us*. New York, NY: Riverhead, 2009. Print.

Pink, Daniel H. *A Whole New Mind: Why Right-Brainers Will Rule the Future*. New York: Riverhead, 2006. Print.

Prigogine, Ilya, and Isabelle Stengers. *Order Out of Chaos: Man's New Dialogue with Nature*. Toronto: Bantam, 1984. Print.

Prigogine, Ilya. *The End of Certainty*. New York: Free, 1997. Print.

Seddon, John. *Freedom from Command and Control*. New York, NY: Productivity Press, 2005. Print.

Scherkenbach, William W. *Deming's Road to Continual Improvement*. Knoxville, TN: SPC, 1991. Print.

Walton, Mary. *The Deming Management Method*. New York, NY: Perigee, 1988. Print.

Wheatley, Margaret J. *Leadership and the New Science: Discovering Order in a Chaotic World*. Berrett-Koehler Publishers, Inc., 1999. Print.

Wooden, John, and Steve Jamison. *Wooden on Leadership*. New York: McGraw-Hill, 2005. Print.

Zukav, Gary. *The Dancing Wu Li Masters: An Overview of the New Physics*. New York: Morrow, 1979. Print.

Zukav, Gary. *The Seat of the Soul*. New York: Simon and Schuster, 1989. Print.

Index

Acknowledgements

I'm extremely grateful to both Franklin Page and J. W. Wilson for their advice and guidance in helping me put this book together. Franklin provided the much-needed copyediting and J. W. supplied significant insight and inspiration. Likewise, our website, Sys-Tao.org, was created by Vince Robbins, and credit for the book's cover, graphics, layout and design belong to Carl Brune. Without these four people, the book would not be complete — we did it together.

Thanks are also due to the many associates of Great Plains who worked by my side over the decades: Ed Dyer, Bob Upton, Ben Blake, John Ustas, Don Bischoff, Bill McClure, Rickey Truelove, Johnnie Compton, Mario Nunez, Clayton Sliger, Steve Plumlee, Comanche Thomas, Barry White, Shirley Jackman, Cari Monsey, and especially my brother Henry and my son Web. And to the rest of the Great Plains family, who are too many to name—I hope you're as proud as I am of what we accomplished, and thank you for the many lessons along the way. We truly did it together.

And of course, my immediate family always comes first. They have been my real life's accomplishment. I'd be nothing without my loving wife, Karen, our kids and their families. Thanks for putting up with me while I worked constantly on this crazy project. Sometimes I am sure you thought I liked my work better than you, but of course that is not true. I truly love all of you. I am just a little like that Zen Buddhist quote:

> The master in the art of living makes little distinction between his work and his play, his labor and his leisure, his mind and his body, his education and his recreation, his love and his religion. He hardly knows which is which. He simply pursues his vision of excellence in whatever he does, leaving others to decide whether he is working or playing. To him he is always doing both.

About the Author

In 1980, Bob Browne and his brother raised $7.5 million, borrowed $35.5 million, and orchestrated a leveraged buy-out of the family business—a Coca-Cola bottling plant in Oklahoma City. For the next 32 years, Bob served as the Chairman and CEO of what became known as Great Plains Coca-Cola Bottling Company. At first, he tried to run the company the way he'd been taught in business school—motivation by incentive, management by objectives, and emphasis on shareholder wealth—but he became frustrated with the unreconciled dilemma of "simultaneously serving Main Street while pleasing Wall Street." Business school had no good answer for this one. He didn't know it at the time, but his frustration would send him on a career-long journey to re-examine and subvert those principles of western business that he'd been taught as fact in school.

Over the ensuing decades, Bob transformed Great Plains from one of many regional bottlers into the fifth-largest bottler of Coke products in North America. Under his leadership, Great Plains' Net Asset Utilization (the ratio of Net Sales to the money tied up in property, plant, and equipment) rose to nearly twice the industry standard.

And Coke took notice. Soon, employees from over 100 bottling operations, and from more than 25 countries, were flocking to Great Plains to attend Bob's "Sys-Tao" meetings. In 2012, Bob sold Great Plains to The Coca-Cola Company for $364 million.

In his first book, *Sys-Tao: Western Logic ~ Eastern Flow*, Bob has condensed his experience into a set of principles, laid out anecdotally in his down-to-earth manner, that will be of great interest and aid to any open-minded student of the rapidly changing landscape of business.

Bob lives in Oklahoma City with his wife, Karen.